Praise for

Incomparable

"FINALLY!!!!! Incomparable...Incomparable is a core-shaking triumph that embodies uniqueness! The pornography reference can also be realized in today's societal unraveling of the heinous evil attacking our most innocent, trusting, and youngest population. One is compelled to confront an intensely striking pursuit toward introspection that provides guidance toward a personal journey of heavenly ordained value and purpose."
-Stephanie

"Having gone through major trauma in my life, I thought I had worked through it and gotten a better self-image of who I am. D.A. Vernier's amazing book showed me that I had not fully tapped into the fullness of who I am in the Lord and how much Jesus loves me...ME!
This book is for the individual working through whatever life has thrown at them AND I can also see it being a great guide for small group settings. I can imagine that amount of healing and loving conversation sparked by this book."
-Kim

Incomparable

Reclaiming Your True Value

Rising Above Your Past

D. A. VERNIER

Scripture quotations are labeled accordingly to which translation that they are from.

Some names and identifying details have been changed to protect the privacy of individuals. Some parts of this book are a work of fiction in order to present a parable like parallel for the benefit of the reader.

ISBN: 979-8-9887072-02

*To Mom and Dad, for your unconditional love,
support, encouragement, and belief in me.*

Table of Contents

Stella

Behind a dumpster at the end of the dark alleyway lay a body curled up tightly, a last effort at survival. An icy wind howled through the murky gloom of the winter night. Shivering was no longer effective; she was beyond cold. Ribbons of snow slithered across the ground and swirled around her feet and exposed legs. The scarcely human figure attempted to draw her body tighter against the elements with what little strength she had left. The way the world had treated her then discarded her she may as well have been inside the trash bin. Perhaps it would be warmer in there, she thought. The doors and windows of the surrounding dwellings were shut tight against the cold and darkness. The nameless, faceless people inside were neither aware of the girl's presence, nor would they have cared had they known.

A lone figure rounded the corner and headed down the dark corridor of the alley. He knew she was there. "Stella," he called out. Stella heard nothing save the relentless wind. "Stella," he came again, moving closer with each step. Stella assumed she was succumbing to the cold and hallucinating. She had not heard her real name in years. But now she recognized the sound of footsteps. Why would anyone be out on a night like this? And why would they be coming down this dead-end alleyway? There was nothing here but a brick wall. The steps grew closer. She was not imaging this. There was indeed somebody moving towards her.

He hovered directly over her now. Stella had neither the strength nor the will to fight, to run, or for that matter, to even open her eyes. Then she heard the strangers tender voice, "Oh Stella, what have they done to you?" The stranger's jaw then tightened. His eyes burned with a fearsome fury. He then uttered in a low voice, "I'll deal with them later." This statement was so resolute that it was undeniable whoever it was directed at would soon suffer greatly for what they had done to Stella. Make no doubt about it.

Those fierce, fiery eyes softened as the figure they belonged to knelt down beside Stella. "It's time to come home my little one," he said as he lifted her frail frame to his. The warmth of his body instantly drove out the aching cold of the bitter air. The protective strength of his arms as he cradled her nearly caused Stella to sob uncontrollably, yet a smile she could not comprehend thwarted her breakdown and filled her with peace. Though she had never laid eyes on this man before, she knew him. As he carried her out of the alley, Stella asked in a barely audible voice, "Where are we going?"

"We're going home where they can never hurt you again," came the reply. And then they were gone.

While the story above is fictional, Stella was a very real person. She lived in an orphanage in Moldova in Eastern Europe. She is said to have had a gleam in her eye and a strong spirit. Though she had some disabilities, she was not hindered by them and had artistic talent. Unfortunately, orphanages like this one can only house so many children and residents are forced out on the streets with no money, no family, and no future, when they "age out" of the orphanages at 16 years old. Many of these girls, including Stella, fall prey to predatory members of the sex trade. They literally become slaves to this hideous industry, where they are beaten and drugged and raped while they serve as sources of revenue for their masters. Stella died at the age of 19 of AIDS. However, her spirit lives on today in houses called Stella's House where girls can seek refuge, get an education, learn life skills, and avoid a life of prostitution and slavery.

No one deserves such treatment as Stella and other girls like her. No one! This book was written to share that truth with you and to introduce you to the protector in the tale above and describe the infinite, immeasurable value he has placed upon you - a value no one can afford and no one can ever take from you.

Chapter 1:
Priceless

The old man leaned on his cane as he slowly rummaged through an assortment of items at the estate sale. With an air of indifference, he tottered past old picture frames, antique lamps, dishes, and ragged old clothing too threadbare to be of use to anybody. He wondered why some of the stuff was even for sale. Who would want such items that had long outlived their use? But then again, wasn't that how younger people viewed him: old, useless, possessing nothing of importance or interest?

One particular section of items did, however, capture the old man's attention. Artwork. There were cracked vases that had once held gardens of beautiful flowers and statuettes that had adorned entry ways to homes, admired by too many people to count. Now these statues lay discarded, piled in boxes with other creations that had seen better days. *What a shame*, the old the man thought. With proper care these beautiful handiworks could have brought joy and beauty to this world for generations to come. Even now, with a little cleaning and polish, they could be restored to their previous splendor. But for whatever reason, they had been tossed aside by their previous owners, one step shy of the trash heap, never to be admired by another human soul. How tragic.

A slight twinkle developed in the old man's eyes as he caught sight of stacks of old paintings: oils and watercolors, landscapes, portraits, and abstracts. His step quickened as he made a bee-line towards this treasure trove of beauty and inspiration. He was partial to paintings as he himself had once been a painter. He still dabbled in this art form, but his vision and dexterity had deteriorated with time, leaving him unable to create works like he had when he was a younger man. In fact, many of his paintings had been quite good, a few even extraordinary. Some had sold for a tidy profit in years past. It was always difficult to part with a painting as he viewed his creations like one of his children. Once a painting was sold, he would lose track of it since it belonged to its new owner. He wondered where they were now. Hanging in someone's foyer or perhaps, even a museum? The old man laughed to himself at that last thought. That would be too much to ask. Who was he to have one of his paintings grace the wall of a museum where people would pause to admire his work?

After studying all the various paintings, appreciating each one for its own merit and beauty as only an artist could, he laid the last one down and began to leave. Then out of the corner of his eye he noticed another frame. Had he missed one? Sure enough, there was one more painting left to admire. As he moved closer, he sensed a familiarity about this painting. Why would he recognize it, he wondered. The wooden frame was weathered and chipped and the canvas was covered with decades of dust, marred by years of mistreatment and neglect. As he lifted the painting for closer inspection and gently brushed the dust from the canvas, he froze. The old man stared in disbelief. That was his signature in the bottom right corner. This painting was his! For a moment he smiled at having found one of his paintings after so many years. But then his joy turned to sadness and a tear inched down his cheek at the thought

PRICELESS

of someone treating one of his paintings, indeed, one of his children, with such neglect and disrespect, discarding it like rubbish. How could anyone not see the individual worth in this painting and take the time to care for it and display it so others could also enjoy its splendor and be inspired by its beauty?

The old man's jaw tightened in anger and resolve. He would not stand for this. He would buy back the painting, restore it and display it with the reverence it deserved. He no longer shuffled as he caringly cradled the tattered work of art and carried it to the clerk's table. There was a new steadiness and purpose in his stride. No price would be too high for him to pay to recover this work of his. He settled up with the estate administrator and hurried home with his treasure.

Over the next several weeks the aged artist lovingly and carefully cleaned and restored his painting with an adroitness and nimbleness his fingers had not known for years. When he was finally done, when he knew the painting was fully returned to its former splendor, he stood back, and with a new found brightness in his eyes, he admired the true magnificence of his artwork as only its creator could. He saw every subtle nuance and brush stroke that made the work special and precious in its own right. He had also rebuilt the frame to fully compliment his creation. Finally, the old man placed the painting on a wall in the foyer of his home where everyone who entered would see it and gaze upon its beauty. And as a final act of respect for his work, the old man vowed he would accept no price, no amount of money for his painting ever again. It was priceless and would remain in his home where it belonged, forever.

YOU ARE GOD'S PRICELESS PAINTING.

If you haven't already guessed where I am going with this story, I will explain. If the analogy is obvious to you please indulge me as I elaborate. The old man in the story represents God, the ultimate artist if you will, the creator of everything. God created the awe-inspiring snow packed peaks of the tallest mountains and covers the valley floors with an indescribable tapestry of flowers every spring. He made the seemingly bottomless oceans yet commanded them to only come so far onto the shore. God paints the sunsets with a palate of colors Monet could never have envisioned. And God's crowning achievement is you! He created all human beings including you. Every person currently living on this earth, every person who previously lived on this earth, and every person yet to be born is so unique and individual that there is, was, and never will be anyone like them. They are one of a kind. *You* are one of kind. There never was nor will there ever be another person like you. And that brings us to the other analogy in the story. While the aged artist represents God, the painting represents you.

Just like the old man in the tale, God created you with such care and attention to detail as to make you one of a kind, a priceless work of art.

For you formed my inward parts
You wove me in my mother's womb

PRICELESS

I will give thanks to You, for I am fearfully and wonderfully made;
Wonderful are Your works,
And my soul knows it very well.
My frame was not hidden from You,
When I was made in secret,
And skillfully wrought in the depths of the earth;
Your eyes have seen my unformed substance;
And in Your book were all written
The days that were ordained for me,
When as yet there was not one of them.

Psalms 139:13-16 (NASB)

The Bible actually tells us that we are His masterpieces made for very specific purposes in this world:

For we are God's masterpiece. He
created use anew in Christ Jesus, so
we can do the good things he
planned for us long ago.

Ephesians 2:10 (NLT)

He made you and released you into the world. Unfortunately, as in our story, great works of art are not always appreciated by everyone. Indeed, occasionally human beings, God's masterpieces, fall into the hands of those who mistreat His works of art. They mar, damage, and harm His creation. This infuriates God. He will one day deal with those who mistreated His children. But right now, He wants to get His creation back and restore it. The marks and damage to the old man's painting were not the fault of the painting. Damage and marks on God's children due to maltreatment by others are likewise no fault of their own. They did nothing to deserve such abuse and thus share no responsibility or guilt for the results. Let me say that again. **Victims of abuse did nothing to deserve such treatment.**

God wants to restore you. He wants to take you back from this world, care for you, heal the damage that has been done to you, and lovingly, tenderly restore you to the glorious child of God He created you to be. It breaks His heart to see one of His children suffering and broken. And He will restore you if you will only let Him. God created you and, therefore, He is the only one who truly knows how to return you to the splendor He originally created you for.

THERE CAN BE NO VALUE, NO NUMBER ATTACHED TO THE PRICE HE PAID FOR YOU AND ME.

In fact, at one time all of His paintings, His children, were lost in this world. And, just like the old man in our story, God paid to have His art returned to Him. He paid dearly. He paid a life for a life. God paid for you and for me with the life of his very own Son, Jesus Christ, in order to have us returned to Him. God willingly gave up His Son to the world so He could buy back the rest of His children. There can

PRICELESS

be no value, no number attached to the price He paid for you or for me. And He says He will never give us back, not for any price.

> *Nothing in all creation will ever be able*
> *to separate us from the love of God.*
>
> Romans 8:39 (NLT)

That means you are priceless! And if you let Him, God will take you into His family and eventually home to live with Him where you will be cared for, loved, and properly treated, for all eternity.

> *When everything is ready, I will come*
> *and get you, so that you will always be*
> *with me where I am.*
>
> John 14:3 (NLT)

INCOMPARABLE

Things to Think About

1) Can you believe or accept that you are a masterpiece created by God and that He made you for a purpose?

    Why or why not?

2) What would it mean to you if you were actually viewed as a priceless, one-of-a-kind masterpiece?

    Would that make you feel differently about yourself?

3) Sit back and imagine for a moment that you are truly a one-of-a-kind masterpiece. What does that feel like?

4) What is it that you don't like about yourself?

    What if those things were actually planned characteristics that add to your value rather than the flaws you think they are?

Chapter 2:

A Word on Abuse

This is a delicate subject. One better left to experts. I am not an expert. Conversely, I was raised by the best parents ever to exist. Sure, I have a biased opinion. But after comparing my parents to other people's parents I have come to realize without a doubt that my brothers and I won the lottery when it came to being assigned our mother and father. We could not have chosen better had we been allowed. I was never abused. My parents were two young kids who married for love with the desire to start a family. Unfortunately, or maybe not, they had difficulty having children for the first 8 years of their marriage. There was disappointment after disappointment for this young couple trying to have children. So when they finally received us boys, my parents loved us unabashedly, sacrificially, unconditionally. They cared for us, protected us, taught us, and corrected us. Our household was a safe place to discover ourselves and a place where we were accepted for who we were. That gave us a base of self-worth before we set out on our own into the world. We did not know abuse.

That being said, my naiveté' was soon crushed by the harsh realities of this world and the human race. I have met person after person after person who has suffered some form of abuse, be it emotional, physical, or sexual. I assumed such horrific treatment only occurred "somewhere else." But, as Peggy Sue Wells in her book, *The Slave Across the Street,* illustrated, appalling cruelty such as sex slavery can occur anywhere, even upper middle-class America. It can happen right under the noses of loving parents who by all accounts are living the American dream complete with financial success, a strong marriage, and healthy children, just as certainly as it can occur on the other side of the globe.

In addition to events in a book by a person I do not know, personal acquaintances –friends- have shared individual stories of sexual abuse, that more often than not, happened at the hand of a family member. These are wonderful, well-adjusted adults raised in seemingly normal families who carry memories of violation of a personal nature at the hands of someone they trusted. One such friend of mine relayed to me a seemingly inordinate number of people she knew in her own circle of friends who had suffered sexual abuse. The sheer volume of instances she told me about did not seem possible. One morning while having breakfast with another good friend of mine who happens to be a counselor, I shared my concerns that this person might be delusional and, due to her experience with abuse, she might be projecting her reality onto others. In short, I thought she might have a problem. My counselor friend assured me, sadly, that she was not making this stuff up or imagining it. He told me that sexual abuse, among other forms of abuse, was truly as rampant as she was telling me. To this day I am still shocked by that horrible truth. How can we treat someone like that? **How can we violate a person so profoundly and so intimately?** Who do we think we are that we can just steal innocence and dignity from another adult, much less a child, without any thought as to how sacred and valuable and personal those qualities are to that person?

WORD ON ABUSE

Honestly, I don't care to hear the excuses or reasons. Is this something new or has it gone on forever and we simply hear more about it now? I fear the latter may be closer to the truth. If I may get on my soap box for one moment, the prevalence and easy access to lewd images, movies, lyrics, and everyday language does not help eradicate such wicked acts. Take pornography for instance. Many people believe pornography is harmless or a normal part of development in curious males moving into adulthood. A well-known Christian apologist rightly noted that pornography promises momentary fulfillment that is never delivered but continually sought. Ultimately, pornography plants its visions in the recipient's mind and remains there long after the viewer has looked away. The memories may never leave. Rather, it percolates and festers in the psyche, affecting and shaping one's thoughts and, possibly, actions. One is considered a prude in today's culture for holding such a view, but I personally know individuals who have had scenarios acted out on them by viewers of pornography. So, please, feel free to tell them they are overreacting.

It is possible to quote voluminous statistics on the prevalence of abuse of all kinds as well as the toll such acts exact on society. But that would reduce the topic to mere numbers and lists. **Victims of abuse are not mere data.** They are people: human beings with souls and psyches that are profoundly affected and potentially permanently altered. The ripple effect of one act of abuse can continue for generations through the children and other family members of victims. That is why I chose to share personal stories rather than cite figures. Numbers do not reflect pain. The experiences of actual people, however, have the ability to connect with our own emotions and humanity.

It was not your fault.

     As I stated earlier, I am not an expert or a counselor or even qualified to prescribe a healing course for any victim of abuse. But I can tell you with full confidence one truth if you have suffered at the hands of another: It was not your fault. You did nothing to deserve such treatment. The person who stole something so personal from you is an animal. And that animal will one day suffer fitting and just consequences for what they did to you, if they haven't already. How has God cared for His people in the past?

> *"I will take revenge; I will pay them*
> *back. In due time their feet will slip.*
> *Their day of disaster will arrive, and*
> *their destiny will overtake them."*
> Deuteronomy 32:35 (NLT)

God takes the treatment of His children personally:

> *"...when you did it to the least of these*
> *my brothers and sisters, you were*
> *doing it to me."*
> Matthew 25:40 (NLT)

15

WORD ON ABUSE

You, on the other hand, are free from any responsibility for your mistreatment. No one ever deserves sexual assault. You are not to blame. While I am not qualified to offer advice on how to overcome the harmful effects, the God I speak of so often has the ability to not only heal your emotional scars but to make you strong and fearless.

> *He gives power to the weak and*
> *strength to the powerless.*
>
> Isaiah 40:29 (NLT)

> *You will bring justice to the orphans*
> *and the oppressed, so mere people can*
> *no longer terrify them.*
>
> Psalm 10:18 (NLT)

This God I speak of has the power to restore any and all who look to him:

> *God has not given us a spirit of fear and timidity, but of power,*
> *love, and self-discipline.*
>
> 2 Timothy 1:7 (NLT)

Finally, we are told that love can heal all things. What this world classifies as love is not love at all. God's love is perfect. What does perfect love look like? It is unconditional. You can do nothing to earn it and, equally, you can do nothing to lose His love. Perfect love accepts you for who you are. God accepts you for who you are because HE MADE YOU. He made you exactly as you are for a purpose: His purpose. Therefore, *of course* He accepts you for who you are. He made you this way for a reason! And imagine a love where there is no fear. No fear of rejection. No fear of reprisal. No fear of punishment.

[God's] love has no fear, because perfect love expels all fear.
1 John 4:18 (NLT)

Not only will He love you unconditionally and with a purity that is beyond our comprehension, He can enable you to shine that kind of love into other people's lives.

And as we live in God, our love grows more perfect.
1 John 4:17 (NLT)

Imagine being such a positive, healing influence in the life of another. Though someone may have wounded you profoundly and deeply, though it appears they may have stolen something from you that you feel can never be replaced, God can not only truly heal you, He can restore and perfect you to be the person He truly designed you to be before this wicked world put its hooks into you. Through our creator you can shine again, brighter than before, and live a great life, loving others as He promises to love you. How? Keep reading.

Things to Think About

1) Read Psalm 10:18 again:
   You will bring justice to the orphans and the oppressed, so mere people can no longer terrify them.

   What would it feel like if you knew people could no longer terrify you? Would you feel strong, empowered, invincible?

2) Look again at 1 John 4:18:
   [God's] love has no fear, because perfect love expels all fear.

   Do you believe there is such a love where there is no fear? Could such a love really exist?

3) One way to assist healing is to help someone you know who is also trying to heal from abuse or mistreatment.

   Is there something you could do to help them? Could you love them with a love like God's as they attempt to heal?

Chapter 3:

How Can a Good God Allow Evil in the World?

A person can pick up any newspaper, watch any television channel, read any internet site, and quickly conclude there is all manner of bad in this world. Some evil is obvious such as war, murder, and rape. Unmentionable events occur daily around the globe. Other types of wickedness can be more subtle, even accepted. Inattention, unkind words, or neglect, though perhaps not commonly categorized as evil, nonetheless, negatively affect the receiver of such.

What are we to do about the evil in our world? Before we attempt to come up with solutions to the problem, we might want to consider who is responsible for the evil and the bad things that happen to people in this world. So who *is* to blame?

I am.

You are.

(Please know that I am in *no way* making the case that a victim of abuse is responsible for their abuse. I tried to make this point crystal clear in the previous chapter. There is only one person to blame: the abuser. And they deserve to be dealt with according to their actions. This chapter is a commentary on bad behavior and evil *in a general sense.* It seeks to answer why this world is so full of corruption. No victim of abuse is to blame or deserving of their treatment. Never let anyone tell you differently. But why such abuse is allowed to happen, I cannot answer that. I wish I could give you an answer. I wish I could go back in time and make all abuse, sexual and otherwise, not happen in the first place. I am not God, and there are certain things I will not understand in this life, though I will struggle to do so until my dying breath. I wish I had a better answer for you, but I don't. God did not even spare His own Son from horrible abuse and torture at the hands of humans. I don't understand why this world has to be so wicked, but it is. But thankfully this world is not all there is. It is simply a momentary blip in time. We have a time of no pain, or sadness, or illness, or suffering to look forward to. More on that later.)

How can you possibly make such a conjecture, you might ask. Because we are all members of the human race, and humans are the beings that harm and torture and contrive all sorts of horrific treatments of their fellow brothers and sisters in this world. It's not God who does these things.

But I'm kind and gentle and loving towards others, you could argue. I would never hurt or harm anyone. To use a sports analogy, if two or three players have stellar performances during a game, but their team comes up short in the final score, they all lose in the end. The team loses. They all lose because they are part of that team. I realize how drastically I am oversimplifying this issue, but just as membership has its privileges, as they say, so too, membership has its consequences. Thus, we all suffer the consequences of our collective actions.

Perhaps you feel I am being too harsh in my evaluation of the human race. This is not my estimation, however; it is God's conclusion. I was as surprised as the next person when I recently stumbled across a passage of scripture that explains how disappointed God was for having created us. He wanted to wipe the slate clean of us and start all over.

> *"The Lord observed the extent of human wickedness on the earth, and he saw that **everything they thought or imagined was consistently and totally evil**. So the Lord was sorry he had ever made them and put them on the earth. It broke his heart. And the Lord said, "I will wipe this human race I have created from the face of the earth. Yes, and I will destroy every living thing – all the people, the large animals, the small animals that scurry along the ground, and even the birds of the sky. **I am sorry I ever made them.**"* (emphasis added)
> Genesis 6:5-7(NLT)

One translation of these verses states that the human heart is "only evil all the time." (NIV) Only when we come face to face with this reality can we begin to come to grips with it.

There is one line of thinking that queries, if God is so good and loving and caring, then why does He allow evil to persist? Why doesn't He step in and stop it? Like I mentioned earlier, you and I continue to make choices that are harmful over and over again. How many of us have ever tried to quit smoking or overeating or drinking excess alcohol or putting other harmful substances into our bodies? Yet, we continue to make the choice to do harmful things to ourselves, our own bodies. Have you ever known a person in your life – a co-worker, a neighbor, or even a family member – that you truly could not stand being around and you had to make a conscious effort to be civil, not to mention kind, to them? Perhaps you were short with them or ignored them altogether. Maybe you tore them down behind their backs to others. Those are choices that we continue to make: choices to be hurtful rather than loving, not only to others, but to ourselves as well.

We may not have tortured or killed anybody, but what have we done to ease the suffering of others in the world? Do we pad our retirement accounts when there are people in parts of this world without one penny to their name, who will not consume 1 calorie of nutrition today, and who have no shelter to sleep in or clean water to drink? How much of our wardrobe is made by humans working for subsistent level wages or under inhumane working conditions? How many of us care to know the answer to that question? We clearly have an issue with making poor choices that are not in keeping with how God intends us to treat one another. So no one is blameless.

I once heard an illustration regarding this question of why God doesn't step in to stop the evil in this world. I cannot recall the source and I ask for forgiveness for not giving proper credit to whom it is due. Following is my attempt to paraphrase this story:

There was a man who was infuriated with God over the state of the world. He had many questions he wanted to ask God, such as why He allowed evil in the world and how a loving God could refuse to put an end to human suffering. One night he got that chance. The man lay down in his bed and fell into a deep sleep. God came to him in a dream that night. God said, "I hear you have some issues with me regarding this world and would like to ask me some questions."

"Indeed I do!" retorted the man. "How can you say you are a loving God when you allow your own children to suffer so?"

"How do you mean?" inquired God.

"Well for starters," growled the man, "how about the state of the world? There are dictatorships and political corruption that leave millions of people in hopeless destitution and persecution. And hunger in the world," he continued. "How can you allow people you say you love to die the slow painful death of starvation? And cancer! Childhood cancer!" he roared, his anger reaching a crescendo. "How could a good God allow an innocent child to suffer with cancer?" the man screamed in consternation.

God looked the man in the eye and lovingly delivered the painful truth. "I sent you a great leader who would have won the Nobel Prize for his plan for world peace, but he died on the battlefield of one of your wars. There was a brilliant young man I sent you who, had he been allowed to become a scientist, would have discovered a way to grow food in arid regions of the earth, forever ending world hunger. He was killed as a child in the crossfire of a drive-by shooting in one of your neighborhoods. Finally, I sent you a brilliant woman who would unlock the cure for cancer. But a doctor killed her in her mother's womb before she ever had a chance to be born."

The man dropped his face into his hands and wept bitterly. He now saw that God was not the reason for evil and suffering in the world, rather He is the solution to and our salvation from this world and ourselves.

Why does God continue to allow such things to continue to happen? Because you and I continue to do wicked things. But what about natural disasters and diseases that humans have no hand in? God originally placed us in paradise, but our choices landed us in the world in which we now find ourselves. Those are the most brutally honest, succinct answers I can provide to the age-old questions that have plagued mankind for eons: Why is there evil in the world and how could a loving God allow it?

Only when we come to grips with the fact that we ourselves as a race are responsible for the mess we find ourselves in, can we begin to see our way out of it. Our wicked ways and selfish choices are responsible for the suffering in the world we so loath and attempt to blame on God. He is not the perpetrator nor the enabler of continued evil, but rather the solution to our woeful condition. God came to save us from ourselves and our nature. If only we would give Him a chance and consider how He would have us treat one another, with selfless love and kindness. Maybe then we could bring about a change to our little sphere of influence in history and this world. Ah, but don't lose hope. There is a way out. John tells us that "every child of God defeats this evil world." (1 John 5:4 NLT) I will share more on that later.

Things to Think About

1) Have you ever wondered why there is evil in the world or why a good God would allow it?

   Does anything you just read about God's nature and the nature of humans change your thinking about evil? Why or why not?

2) Is there anything you could change about how you treat people on a day-to-day basis that would make a positive difference in their lives? Write those things down.

3) Would you do just one of the things you listed in question #2 to one person today?

4) What are your thoughts about 1 John 5:4: ... *"every child of God defeats this evil world."* What would it mean to you to defeat this evil world?

Chapter 4:

Forgiveness

Forgiveness. An easy word to say, but a difficult concept to live out, especially when you are the one who is supposed to offer it. When we want someone to forgive *us* after we have wronged them it is very easy for us to ask them to extend forgiveness to us. We may even desire their forgiveness so much that we beg them to forgive us. We can't have peace until they say those three words: I forgive you. But when the shoe is on the other foot, and we are the ones who have been mistreated, cheated, fooled, lied to, _____, (fill in the blank) and someone asks us to grant them forgiveness, it can be a very different story. They may have hurt us very deeply and now they want us to say we forgive them and move on with our lives as if everything were back to normal and the offense never occurred. What if we are not ready to forgive? What if we want to see a little more remorse from the person who hurt us? Perhaps we would like to see them pay for their offense. Maybe we would like a little revenge or we want to hold this over their head a little while longer so they can get a sense of how we felt when they hurt us. What do we do then?

People ask for forgiveness, and people grant forgiveness to others. But what does that really mean? Is it just a word we say or does something else happen when we forgive someone? Merriam-Webster defines forgiveness as *the act of giving up resentment or ceasing to feel resentment against an offender.* Read that definition again. It says that, as the one granting forgiveness, *we* eliminate resentment. *We* give it up. *We* get rid of it. Resentment is a heavy, bitter load to carry. This definition affirms that we get rid of something very negative in our life when we forgive someone. (Hold onto that thought for later.) So what does God have to say about forgiveness?

> *Remember, the Lord forgave you, so you must forgive others.*
> Colossians 3:13

> *If you forgive those who sin against you, your heavenly Father will forgive you. But if you refuse to forgive others, your Father will not forgive your sins.*
> Matthew 6:14-15

> *...forgive anyone you are holding a grudge against, so that your Father in heaven will forgive your sins, too.*
> Mark 11:25

> *[forgive] one another, just as God through Christ has forgiven you.*
> Ephesians 4:32

Notice that in each of these verses our act of forgiveness is tied to the fact that we have been forgiven. This is a reminder to us so we don't lose sight of the truth that we have been granted forgiveness in case we are contemplating not extending this courtesy to another person. **God forgave us first when we were in dire need of forgiveness.** So who do we think we are when we consider not forgiving another person when we ourselves have been forgiven of any and all wrongs we have committed or will commit?

"I can lift my hand, but you supply the feeling."

In the book, *The Shack,* the main character, Mack, is arguing with a female character about how God allows evil to occur in this world. Mack does not agree with how God can forgive people who have committed heinous acts. So the female character places Mack in God's shoes and puts him in charge of casting judgement on people.

Earlier in the book, Mack's little daughter had been murdered. The woman asks Mack what should happen to the man who killed his daughter. Mack, in no uncertain terms, makes known that his daughter's murderer should burn in hell and suffer for all eternity for what he did. The woman then does something very powerful. Since Mack appears quite comfortable casting judgement on people, the woman demands that Mack judge his remaining children. She tells Mack that only three of his children can go to heaven and the other two will go to hell. Mack's job is to decide which of his children get to go to heaven and which go to hell for all of eternity. Mack's countenance changes as he is visibly distraught by this task. He tells the woman there is no way he can make that decision. She tells him he has to, since he feels he knows better than God. He continues to try to get of out making this decision, but she will not allow him to. She in essence tells him, "Decide! Do it! NOW!"

The main character finally breaks down and admits he cannot allow any of his children to suffer such torment and that he will take their place in hell. He will pay the penalty for them so they don't have to suffer. The woman then explains that Mack now understands how God dealt with the prospect of any of His children going to hell. He sent his own Son to take our punishment for us. And as God's Son suffered horrendously on that cross -as He was mocked, as He was punched and whipped and spit on - Jesus asked His Father to forgive the very people who were torturing Him. Jesus had that much love for them. For us. That is what God's forgiveness looks like.

Corrie ten Boom was the daughter of a Dutch watchmaker during World War II. Corrie and her family were arrested by the Gestapo for hiding Jews in their home. Corrie and her sister Betsy eventually ended up in a Nazi concentration camp where Betsy died. Corrie was eventually released through what has been rumored to be a clerical error. One week after Corrie's release from Ravensbruck, all the women in her age group were sent to the gas chambers.

After the war Corrie would go on to write and speak about her experiences. In 1947 while speaking to a group in Munich, Germany on the topic of forgiveness, Corrie used an analogy of God casting our sins into a deep ocean to demonstrate that He no longer even *remembers* our sins once they are forgiven. Hebrews 10:17 says, "Their sins...I will remember no more." After her speech as the

FORGIVENESS

crowd filed out of the room, one man came forward to speak with Corrie. He did not recognize Corrie but she definitely recognized him. This very man had been one of the cruel Nazi prison guards at the concentration camp Corrie was sent to and where her sister died. Who can understand the emotion she felt as the memories of walking naked in front of this man and other guards along with the other women in this prison camp came rushing back to her? Yet here stood this very man directly in front of her. Not only was he face to face with one of his victims, the former guard commented on Corrie's talk on forgiveness saying he was now a Christian and he knew God have forgiven him for the cruel acts he committed against women when he was a prison guard. Then he extended his hand to Corrie and asked if she would forgive him.

Corrie could not take the man's hand. She could not forgive this man. She could not, would not give up her resentment and hatred for the treatment she and her sister suffered at his hands. Yet here she stood, having just spoken about the need for others to forgive those who have wronged them, but unable to extend that forgiveness herself. At that moment Corrie, convicted of her own hypocrisy, called out to Jesus as she reluctantly lifted her hand to place it into the outstretched hand of the guard and prayed, "I can lift my hand, but you supply the feeling." She goes on to say that God indeed provided healing for her in that moment. She talks of a release of resentment and hatred that can only be explained by God's power acting within her. Corrie admits she could not forgive this man. She required God to do it and she explains how he did it: ..."he has given us the Holy Spirit to fill our hearts with his love." Romans 5:5 In the same way, we all require God's power to supply us with the love to forgive those who have horribly hurt us and wronged us, because, "What is impossible with men is possible with God." Luke 18:27

Forgiveness benefits us as well as those we forgive.

So if forgiveness is sometimes impossible for us, why even attempt to forgive truly awful people for truly awful acts? Because our forgiveness benefits *us* as well as those we forgive. Remember the dictionary definition that described forgiveness as the act of giving up resentment? Resentment and bitterness eat away at *us*, not the other person. If we harbor such emotions *we* are the ones being harmed, not our offender. In other words, long after the offense, we are still allowing ourselves to be victimized by the person who originally harmed us. Let me emphasize that again: *we* now have control over whether the victimization continues or ends! We have the power to end the pain. We have the power to get rid of the burden we carry. That person can only continue to harm us if *we* allow them to. They no longer have any power over you if you chose not to allow them to. You are in control, not them.

Forgiveness is not necessarily a feeling, but rather, an act of will. **You may not *feel* like forgiving the other person, but you can *choose* to forgive them for your benefit as much as theirs. When you choose to forgive them, you release their hold on you.** You dump the negative emotions of resentment and bitterness and anger and hatred. Initially, forgiveness may simply be you uttering the words, "I forgive you." There may be no feeling of compassion for the other person. But if you, by an act of your will, choose to forgive someone because you realize God's way is better than yours, He will provide the feeling in time. Nevertheless, you can take a step in that direction by consciously choosing to offer forgiveness to another person even if you don't feel like doing it initially. You may have to utter those words, "I forgive you," over and over and over again. Depending on the depth of violation against you, it may take some time to fully come to a place where you feel you have actually forgiven a person, but when you show God you trust Him and take a step in His direction, He will not let you down.

But what if the other person will not accept your forgiveness or does not feel they did anything requiring your forgiveness? Not your problem. You only have control of your own thoughts and actions. You will benefit from releasing your feelings of anger and resentment. If they chose not to accept your forgiveness, that is their problem, not yours. The same thing goes if the person you are forgiving has died. You can still release the grip they have on you. You can still get out from under the cloud of resentment and bitterness hanging over you. Through your sheer act of will and God's Spirit working within you, you can experience healing from past transgressions by others. *You* can choose to be free and healed. *You* are in control now, not your offender.

Things to Think About

1) Write down any feelings you may have toward someone who has hurt you. Be as honest and graphic as you like with these feelings.

2) Now look at that list.

   How many of those feelings have any effect on the person you are angry with?

   How many of those feelings affect you?

3) Would you like to get out from under those negative feelings and emotions? Would you like to be free from those feelings? Would you like to be free from the other person?

   Fill in the person's name at the end of this statement: **I forgive _____.**

   Repeat this phrase to yourself over and over again throughout the day and the days to come. Each time you do, ask God to help you forgive this person. Ask him to replace

FORGIVENESS

the old feelings of resentment with feelings of peace and
forgiveness. Ask God to free you from this person.

4) Picture yourself as the one in control now. See yourself in
your mind as the one who decides whether or not this
person has any power over you.

Picture yourself as strong and proclaim definitively, **"They
do NOT have power over me! I forgive _____ and I am
free from them forever!"**

Run this image through your mind everyday – many times
every day – until you finally believe the truth: You are free
from them because you are in control now!

Chapter 5:

How Does God See You?

Young Kylie twirled and danced in the sunshine with all the energy and exuberance a 4-year-old could muster. She paused for a moment to study a butterfly that had landed nearby. Then she was off again, laughing and skipping – truly the happiest child in the world. And why wouldn't she be? It was a gorgeous spring day and all she had on her agenda was to play in the park with her father who sat nearby beaming at his beautiful daughter. In his eyes she was perfect. He would change nothing about her. Not her hair color, her height, her personality and definitely not that smile. Little Kylie could melt the hardest of hearts with that precious, joyful smile.

By the world's standards, though, Kylie was far from perfect. She had been born with some facial disfigurements. The world could be so cruel and short-sighted, thought her father. Why couldn't people get past the outer imperfections and see the beauty within this darling soul? But that was fine by him. He would protect her. Indeed, little Kylie was unaware of how the world viewed her. All she knew about her appearance was what she saw in her daddy's eyes. They gleamed with awe when he looked at her. When Kylie looked into her father's eyes she knew without a doubt she was the most magnificent little girl on the face of the earth and would be forever loved by her daddy.

How we view ourselves is often shaped, at least in part, by how others see us. Right or wrong, good or bad, others' opinions affect our concept of worth as individuals. Parents, friends, co-workers, bosses – many people we come in contact with – have an effect on how we see ourselves. Do we see ourselves as good, as having little value, smart or stupid, beautiful or ugly? We do not come up with these views purely on our own. Many people shape our self-concept. While we cannot control the views of others, we definitely control our own thoughts and beliefs about our inner person, our outward appearance, our self-worth, our worthiness of love and respect, and our ability to contribute to this world and the human race. What is imminently important is to determine if our view of ourselves is correct and justified. Is it healthy? If not then we need to correct it if we want to live a happy and constructive/fulfilling life. Our view of ourselves can be elevated, even narcissistic, or it can be mistakenly low. Either extreme is inaccurate and can negatively affect how we function and treat ourselves and others. So where do we go to get an objective view of who we are and our worth?

Imagine you are sitting quietly in an art gallery in front of a famous painting. Let's use the *Mona Lisa* as an example. You are settled comfortably in a chair far enough from the painting so other visitors don't notice you but close enough that you can hear their conversations. One person may walk up to the painting and be able to explain to their companion when the work was painted and what was going on in history at that time. Another person may be able to expound on what was happening in the artist's life at the time he painted this particular work. There may be someone who can explain at length the use of light and shapes and other artistic tricks of the trade that make this painting special. Perhaps a couple visitors might even discuss the type of paint used in the production of the painting, how it was made, and what it consisted of. An expert from the gallery would be able to explain the art form employed by the artist in this particular painting. But one thing would be glaringly clear after you listened to all these different people and experts discuss this painting: only the artist knows *why* he created this painting.

We have already established you are a masterpiece, created by a master artist who has determined your worth to be incalculable. But perhaps we should ponder why He created us in the first place. Only He knows for sure. It would be impossible, arrogant, and foolish for me to pretend to know the mind of God. This is a topic of never-ending conversation and speculation. However, God has left a few clues in his book, the Bible, as to why He created humans. The Bible tells us He made us similar to Himself, and He created us to be good stewards of this earth. He made us so we would produce offspring that would also honor Him and further reflect His image. There are some scholars that posit a theory that we were created with some deep metaphysical battle in mind between Satan, other fallen angels, and God, but that is way above my cerebral capacity. One verse however, provides perhaps the simplest description of why God created humans; He made us for His own purposes. (Proverbs 16:4) He has His reasons. He is God and we may not be able to fully comprehend His lofty reasons. More importantly however, the very fact that God made you means:

1) You have value
2) You have a purpose

HOW DOES GOD SEE YOU?

The lyrics to a particular country song state, "All I really gotta do is live and die." What? How crazy is that! Imagine if all you did after being born was to simply exist until you died. What a waste! You have been put here for so much more than that. God had a purpose for making us and He has a purpose for each of our lives. Our job is to seek that out then live out that purpose to the best of our ability. Does everyone's purpose have to be some lofty undertaking that will make a widely known difference such as discovering the cure for cancer? No. Of course not. There are so many heroes we will never hear of who have made a difference in the life of one person, but just because their contribution is not widely known does not make it any less important.

You Have Value

You are valuable. You have worth. **Because God created you, *you* have extreme value.** When Jesus Christ walked this earth He would teach His followers by using short lessons called parables in order to help them better understand what He was trying to teach them. He used three such parables to teach people about their unfathomable value in His and God's eyes. In one example, Jesus told the story of a woman who lost a coin. At that time and in that region of the world a woman would receive 10 coins as a wedding gift. Imagine how she would feel if she lost one of those coins. She would turn on all the lights in the house, get down on her hands and knees, and scour that house, turning it upside down until she found that one coin even though she had 9 others just like it. That one coin held so much value and was worth so much to her that she would search high and low until she found it. Christ says that is how valuable you are to Him. If you are lost, He wants you back. Even though there are many people who know Him and believe in Him and belong to Him, you are so valuable to Him He will relentlessly pursue you to get you to join His family.

In another parable Jesus uses a shepherd to describe our worth to Him. Picture a sheep herder who has 100 sheep. To a sheep farmer his sheep are his most valuable assets. If one comes up missing, that shepherd will leave the other 99 to go look for that one missing sheep. When he finds it, he will place it on his shoulders and carry it back to the rest of the herd. He will tell all his friends how he found his lost sheep and wants them to celebrate, to throw a huge party with him because he is so excited over having all his sheep back in one place. Again, Christ tells us that is how all of heaven celebrates when one of its lost children returns to the family. We are that valuable to God.

You have unimaginable value in God's
eyes.

And finally, there is the story of the prodigal son. Most everyone has heard this story in one form or another, but let's revisit it here. The word prodigal is defined as being very wasteful with money, spending it recklessly like there is no end to it. So this parable is about a man who has two sons. One son wants his inheritance immediately, before his father is even dead. The father honors his request and the son takes off to the big city for some wild partying. This son lives high-on-the-hog, lavishly spending his inheritance until he has blown it all. Now what is he supposed to do? At his lowest point he takes a job feeding pigs. He is so hungry at one point that Jesus says he craved the food he was feeding to the pigs. The son finally realizes that his father's servants have more than enough food to eat. So he decides he will return home and beg his father for a job so he can have food to eat.

The boy's father has been missing him dearly ever since he left, as only a father could. When the father looks to the horizon and sees his son in the distance, he is ecstatic to see his son returning home. He jumps up excitedly and tells his servants to arrange a huge party for his son's return. Before his son even has a chance to grovel before his father to ask for a job as a servant his father sprints out to him and hugs him in a huge loving embrace. The father is so happy to have his son back in the family that all is forgotten. That is how God sees us. No matter what we have done, how far we have strayed, or how long we have been absent from Him, He is telling us through this parable that He will welcome us back if we return to Him. You have worth. You have unimaginable value in God's eyes. That is what real love looks like.

God Has a Purpose For You

How could God have a purpose for me? I am so unimportant. There is nothing special about me, you may think. Well we just established that you have worth and value that cannot be measured, so that line of thinking is not correct. Plus, God has a history of telling people of the purposes He has for them. When His people, the Israelites, were enslaved, He encouraged them to stay strong and hopeful by telling them, "...I know the plans I have for you...They are plans for good and not for disaster, to give you a future and a hope." (Jeremiah 29:11) How awesome would it be if we discovered that God has plans for our future, to give us hope?

There is a story told of a little boy who was walking on a beach littered with thousands of live starfish that had washed up on the shore during a storm. Moving down the beach with resolve, the little boy would bend down, pick up a starfish, and put it back into the water so it could swim away to safety. He did this over and over again. An older gentleman watched the boy from a distance for a while, dumbfounded by the boy's actions because there were so many beached starfish. It was impossible for the boy to rescue them all. Finally, the old man confronted the boy, asking him incredulously, "What do you think you are doing? There are so many starfish washed up on the shore. There is no way you can rescue all of them. You are not even making a difference with the few starfish you have tossed back into the water." The little boy bent down, gently picked up a stranded starfish, placed him back into the safety of his ocean home, and looked up at the old man as he replied, "It made a difference to that one." Then the little boy continued undeterred down the beach rescuing more starfish. You see, you only have to discover and follow *your* purpose and make a difference in the life or lives of those you were created to be of help to in order to be a true success in life.

God is looking for people who desire
to live for Him and accomplish what
He wants to accomplish.

There needs to be a distinction made here regarding different sorts of purposes. We may already feel we have a purpose whether it be making loads of money, living in a big house, having a family, etc. But those types of purposes will die when we die. Those are self-centered purposes, possibly even selfish. If we seek out God's purpose for us, however, that type of purpose will follow us even after we leave this earth. God's purpose is to grow his kingdom with people who love Him and whom He loves. God is looking for people who desire to live for Him and accomplish what He wants to accomplish. Such a purpose is so much bigger than our own individual self. Such a purpose is far more meaningful than a self-absorbed purpose, and it is eternal. There is a saying that states a person who is wrapped up in themselves is a small package. Why not be part of something larger, something that will last forever? That is where God wants to take us. He wants to use each of our individual talents, skills, and passions (which He gave us by the way) to accomplish something bigger than we ever dared imagine. Not only do you have immeasurable worth in God's eyes, but He has plans for you that are beyond anything you have ever conceived.

One final note on your value: if you are still unsure if God sees you as valuable, just look at the price He paid to get you back. That's right. I said He paid to get you back. The price He paid is similar to a ransom or, in Biblical times, the price one would pay to purchase the freedom of a slave. You and I and all of humanity are slaves to something. God wants to free us from our slavery to whatever it is that controls us. In order to accomplish that God paid the most incredibly high price ever paid in the history of mankind. He paid for you and for me with the life of His Son. The price for our freedom was the life of a perfect being. Jesus Christ just happened to be that perfect being. He was wrongly accused by a Roman court, whipped, beaten, tortured and killed. That punishment should have been yours and mine. But Christ took it for us.

Imagine you are in prison as punishment for crimes you actually committed. Now imagine the jailer comes to your cell one day, swings the door open wide, and tells you that you are free to go. Someone paid your bail and your sentence has been commuted. What do you do? Do you tell the jailer, "No, I am going to stay here in this prison cell?" Or do you run out of that prison as fast as you can and find the person who paid your fine, a fine you could never have afforded, and thank them profusely? That is the situation every one of us as members of the human race are faced with in this life. Christ paid our fine to free us from this life of making wrong decisions over and over and over again. We can choose to stay right where we are in our prisons, or we can reach out and accept His gift of freedom from the ways of this world, from ourselves. It's your choice. Whatever your decision, this will always remain true: God paid an immeasurable amount for you because He sees you as immeasurably valuable. And why shouldn't He? He created you, and He knows precisely what your worth is.

HOW DOES GOD SEE YOU?

Things to Think About

1) Are you hindered by bad decisions and bad habits from which you can't seem to break free? Write them down here or somewhere no one else can see. Talk to God about these things you have written down. Pour your heart to Him. Tell Him how you really feel about these things. Then ask Him to help you do something about them, to break free from their hold on your life.

2) Do you feel you have value, worth, and a purpose in this life? Why or why not?

3) In this chapter, we listed three examples of how importantly God views you. He would leave everyone else to come find you. He doesn't have a devious motive for doing this. He just wants you safe, and there is no place safer than with a God who loves you purely.

   Are you able to accept that truth? Why or why not?

Chapter 6:
You Have a Purpose

Since the beginning of time human beings have pondered the question, *What is the purpose of life*? More specifically humans have tried to determine what *their* individual purpose is in this world. What do you think is *your* purpose in life? Do you even think you have one? I bring this up because you – as well as each and every one of God's children – have a specific purpose for being here on this earth. Let me say that again: *You* have a specific purpose in this life. You have been put here for a specific reason with a specific mission to fulfill. I want you to write your name in the blank below.

_____ has a purpose in life!

I want you to say that to yourself every day. I want you to look yourself *in the eye* in the mirror in the morning and recite this to yourself. I want you to remind yourself many, many, many times throughout the day of this truth. (Yes, this is a true statement.) I want you to say this to yourself before you fall asleep at night. I want you to say it over and over and over again until you truly believe it. I don't want you to fake it. I want you to really believe this statement with all your heart and mind. I want you to be so sure of this fact that nothing can make you doubt it again.

I once heard a pastor teach about the story of Christ's entry into Jerusalem the week before He died. It is called the triumphal entry because He was seen as a king by the people of the city as He entered into Jerusalem. He rode into town on a young donkey as people shouted His praise and declared Him King.

This young donkey that Jesus rode into town on had never been ridden before. But it was much more than just another baby donkey. It was the firstborn male donkey of its mother. In Jewish tradition, the firstborn male animal was to be sacrificed to God because it belonged to Him. However, God made a way for people to "buy back" a firstborn male animal: a lamb or young goat would have to be sacrificed in the place of the donkey. According to this tradition, if this male donkey was not bought back, its neck had to be broken. (Exodus 13:13) Thus, this young donkey that Christ rode on was only alive because another animal had been killed in its place. Therefore, it had great value. But, even though it was valuable it had not yet been used. It had yet to realize its full potential. In fact, Jesus' disciples found it tied to a post, not doing anything useful for anyone. They untied the young donkey and brought it to Jesus. Jesus in turn rode into Jerusalem on this baby donkey as people shouted praises to Him and threw palm branches down in front of the donkey for it to walk upon. (This is where we get the tradition of Palm Sunday.) The people were witnessing the arrival of a King; that is why they showered Jesus with praise and adulation.

This donkey was valuable. It had been spared because the life of another animal had been given in its place. However, its true value and purpose were not realized until somebody unchained the restraint that held it to the post so it could be useful to someone. A King, Jesus Christ, was in need of this seemingly lowly donkey. He had a task - a purpose - for it to fulfill. But once the donkey had served its purpose for Christ, what did Jesus do with it then? He sent it back home so it could be useful to others.

So why do I tell you this story? How does it relate to you? You and I are the young donkey tied to a post in the story. We have value; we are alive, only because someone else was sacrificed in our place. We were doomed because of our wicked, evil hearts we read about earlier. We were headed for punishment. But Christ stood in our place and took our punishment for us when He was killed through crucifixion at the hands of executioners. **That was supposed to be us! We were supposed to be punished! We were supposed to suffer and die!** But Christ took that punishment for us. That must mean we are incredibly important and valuable to Him.

And just like in the case of that donkey that was spared, Jesus has a job for us, a purpose. You may feel you are too unimportant to be of use to Christ. (Unfortunately, this world puts that thought in a lot of our minds.) But Jesus is very different from this world. He turns things upside down. What the world considers useless, Jesus finds very useful. What the world tosses to the curb as trash, Jesus takes home as valuable treasure. You see, in Jesus' day, a conquering king would never ride into town on a baby donkey. He would be at the head of the victory parade on a powerful white stallion. But Jesus, the reigning King of the world, rode into Jerusalem on a baby donkey that was fit for a child to ride on.

What is holding you back from being useful? What are you still chained to?

But what had to happen before Christ could use this donkey? It had to be freed from the pole it was tied to. What is holding you back from being useful? What are you still chained to? Your past? Guilt? A low opinion of yourself? An addiction? Jesus can just as easily free you from whatever is holding you back as He freed that young donkey from a post so many years ago.

The final lesson from this story is what happened to the donkey after its value was realized. Did Jesus keep it for Himself? Nope. He sent it back home to where it came from so it could continue to be useful there. That was its purpose. You don't have to be what the world considers a "superstar" to be useful in Christ's family. You simply have to be willing to serve Him and others with your unique purpose RIGHT...WHERE...YOU...ARE. You might be a great mother that can raise young children into awesome adults that will further benefit the people of this world. You may have the gift of teaching. Perhaps you aspire to the fields of health care or law or cleaning or the service industries. **Whatever you are uniquely wired to do, you can be valuable to so many people right where you currently are.** You just have to be willing to acknowledge your value, discover your purpose in this life, and pursue that purpose by using it to help others.

Discovering Your Gifts

When we belong to God's family we are blessed with certain gifts.

God has given us different gifts for doing certain things well. So if God has given you the ability to prophesy, speak out with as much faith as God has given you. If your gift is serving others, serve them well. If you are a teacher, teach well. If your gift is encouraging others, be encouraging. If it is giving, give generously. If God has given you leadership ability, take the responsibility seriously. And if you have a gift for showing kindness to others, do it gladly.

Romans 12:6-8

Your gift is individually yours. Don't worry about what others are good at. Focus on what you are good at. You can play a badly needed, unique role in this world and in the life of others. Imagine if everyone was good at being a leader. Who would they lead? What if everyone was gifted to be a house painter? Who would design or build the houses for them to paint**? Don't try to be anyone other than who you were designed to be.** Embrace your individual design and wiring and be good at it. Develop your gift or gifts.

Members of a family all have different personalities, strengths, and things they are good at. Everyone plays a role in a family. The same is true in God's family: we all have a role to fulfill. He has designed us that way for a purpose.

For we are God's masterpiece. He created us anew in Christ Jesus, so we can do the good things he planned for us long ago.

Ephesians 2:10

Do you see how we have come full circle from the beginning of the book when you first read that you were a priceless masterpiece?

YOU HAVE A PURPOSE

God has made you distinctly unique from anyone else because He has specific things He wants you to do.

A light bulb may have gone off for some of you. You may know precisely how you have been gifted. Others may not be so sure. Don't despair. You can begin figuring out your gifts by asking yourself a few questions. What have you been good at in the past? What have you been successful at doing? What do you love doing? What activities do you fully enjoy doing? What energizes you to the point that you lose track of time doing it? These questions are a good place to start figuring out how you are wired. There are also spiritual gifts assessment questionnaires online that can aid you in discovering your unique abilities.

There is one area where victims of abuse are uniquely qualified to be of extensive help to others. Horrible things have happened to you that should never happen to anyone. However, you can upend the negative consequences of such treatment and use them for good. The Bible clearly states that God causes everything to work for the good of those who love Him and are called according to his purpose for them. (Romans 8:28) This in *no way* implies that what happened to you is in any way good. What is says is that God can have the last word and turn what happened to you around in the face of your perpetrators.

You can let your experience destroy you or you can punch back at those who harmed you by preventing another victim from falling prey to their wickedness. Your experience gives you a credibility with other victims that no PhD can ever convey. You can help others recover just like you are recovering, because you have been there in their place. Only you can simply sit with or hold a victim of abuse and exude a presence, an understanding, like no one who has never gone through what you have can. You can cause someone whose trust has been shattered to trust again. Your abusers tried to break you. Show them that they actually made you stronger. Make them cower and run when they realize they have actually created a "monster" for good. Their plan backfired. Use your pain to prevent such pain from coming upon another person. Make the abusers sorry they ever messed with you. You have the ability to keep them from getting their hands on other victims. Punch a bully and he runs away crying. Punch away girl, punch away.

3 Things to Know About Yourself

If you can come up with answers to the following three questions, you will have a great jump start on figuring out your purpose in life. The answers to these questions are different for everybody. Don't worry about how others would answer these questions. Focus on yourself.

1) Who are you?

This sounds like a silly question, doesn't it? For the longest time I never quite understood this question. *Who am I? I'm me of course. What a stupid question*. Over the years, however, this question began to make sense to me. When you ask yourself who you are, you are really asking what makes you YOU? What skills and strengths do you possess? What are you good at? What are your likes and dislikes? Are you a morning person or would you prefer to sleep in?

YOU HAVE A PURPOSE

Do you like funny movies or action flicks? Maybe you don't like movies at all. Perhaps you prefer to read. What do you think about? Do you like crowds or just a few friends? Maybe you prefer alone time.

As I just said, the answers to these questions are different for everybody. Don't worry about how others would answer these questions. Focus on yourself. You can't be anybody else but you. Be thankful for that! You wouldn't want to be anybody else. If you were, the world would miss out on you. Let me say that again. If you don't bless the world with who you really are, the human race will be worse off because of that. Don't deprive those around you of the blessing that is YOU. Discover who you really are, the masterpiece God designed you to be, and be awed by your special, unique characteristics that nobody else possesses but you. You truly are amazing. Don't overlook that fact and miss out on enjoying the masterpiece you are.

2) Whose Are You?

Tim Tebow, college football Heisman Trophy winner, professional football and baseball player and, great humanitarian raised this question in his book, *Shaken.* To whom do you belong? Whose are you? If you belong to a sports team you identify as an athlete. If you are a member of a choir, you most likely are a singer. What group or family you belong to tells a lot about you. Let's try a little exercise. What ideas come to your mind if I told you a certain person was a member of the group Doctors Without Borders that provides medical aid in areas of war, natural disasters, or great need? What are your initial thoughts of that person? Now, what if I introduced you to someone and told you they belong to the Nazi party? See how that works?

So, who or what group do you identify with? Whose are you? This question is even more important than who you are because it has eternal consequences. If you are a member of God's family you have some amazing benefits due to that association.

For you are all children of God through faith in Christ Jesus.
Galatians 3:26 (NLT)

... you will be my sons and daughters, says the Lord...
2 Corinthians 6:18 (NLT)

... you are also complete through your union with Christ.
Colossians 2:10 (NLT)

And we have a priceless inheritance – an inheritance that is kept in heaven for you, pure and undefiled, beyond the reach of change and decay.
1 Peter 1:4 (NLT)

...you are a chosen people. You are royal priests... God's very own possession...he called you out of the darkness into his wonderful light.
2 Peter 2:9 (NLT)

Did you get all that? Those who identify with God, who are members of His family, have been hand-picked by Him. He chose you to be one of His children.   And with family membership comes certain privileges. You are made complete through Christ. You are no longer broken or incomplete. You are a royal priest. (Did you ever think anyone would refer to you as a royal priest?) You have a crazy, ridiculous inheritance awaiting you one day that is beyond anything you can imagine. It is set aside, waiting for you. And finally, if you have decided to become a member of God's family, you are God's. You belong to Him. Forever. That's *whose* you are. So what is your answer to that question? Whose are you?

3) Where Are You Going?

There is a story told of Albert Einstein. It is said he boarded a train from Princeton one day and when the conductor got to Dr. Einstein's seat to collect his ticket, Einstein couldn't find it. He checked his coat pocket. No ticket. He checked his trouser pockets. Still no ticket. He looked in his brief case. Same story. Dr. Einstein was on a train with no proof he had purchased a ticket. The conductor, recognizing the well-known genius, said, "It's okay. I believe you bought a ticket." Einstein sheepishly thanked the conductor who then continued on down the train collecting passengers' tickets. Shortly after that, the conductor looked back towards Dr. Einstein's end of the train and noticed Einstein on his knees looking under his seat still trying to locate his ticket. The conductor walked back to the doctor and said, "Dr. Einstein. It's okay. I know who you are." Einstein, looking up from the floor replied, "I know who I am also young man. What I don't know is where I am going."

You have a purpose that others will greatly benefit from you fulfilling.

Where are you going? Do you know what you would like to do in this life? Do you know what type of job or education you would like to pursue? What kinds of friends are you going to surround yourself with? If you would like to one day marry, do you know what kinds of traits you would like your mate to possess? Have you ever thought about such things and even written them down for clarity? It is said that a ship without a destination simply bobs around at sea. That sounds rather pointless, doesn't it?

As you have learned, you are very valuable. You have a purpose that others will greatly benefit from you fulfilling. It is well worth your time to seriously consider who you are, what makes you uniquely you, to whom you belong, and what you would like to do with your precious time and abilities on this earth. Don't waste this beautiful gift you have been given by bobbing aimlessly at sea. How horrible it would be if a priceless work of art, a masterpiece, was kept in a storage room where no person could ever be inspired and awed by its beauty. How horrible it would be if the world never got to experience the priceless masterpiece that is you.

YOU HAVE A PURPOSE

Things to Think About

1) What activities are you good at?
2) What do you love to do so much that you lose track of time doing it and you would do this even if nobody paid you to do it?
3) How would you view your life if it were true that you were extremely valuable and have a purpose to fulfill in this world? What would you do with your future?
4) Fill out the table by following the instructions below.

What do I think of myself?	What does God say about me?

INCOMPARABLE

In the left-hand column list out all the thoughts you have of yourself. How do you view yourself?

Read the following verses: Galatians 3:26, 2 Corinthians 6:18, Colossians 2:10, 1 Peter 1:4, 1 Peter 2:9

In the right-hand column, write out how God sees you. How does He describe you? What promises does He make to you?

Replace any negative opinions you may have of yourself with the truth on the right-hand side of the page.

Chapter 7:
A Beautiful Woman

So what does a real woman look like? Role models can provide helpful examples for us to refer to when attempting to successfully navigate our way through this life. If you are looking to Hollywood, "reality" TV, or women's magazines for role models, however, stop! For the most part those sources depict unrealistic and horrible role models. I feel for ladies who derive their opinion of the ideal woman or what they believe they should look like from the magazines in the grocery store checkout line. I doubt very highly that anything that graces the covers of those periodicals actually exists in nature. I believe it was Cindy Crawford, the supermodel of all supermodels, who confessed that photographers airbrushed her inner thighs in order to make them appear slimmer and boosted her breasts with duct tape during photo shoots. So even Cindy Crawford doesn't look as perfect as her photos depict, and she readily admits that and has expressed concern for women and girls who aspire to attain that level of perfection because it does not exist. So stop using today's magazines and models as your benchmark. There exists a better example and description of what a real woman is like.

It has been said that the Bible is life's instruction manual. That is hardly a comprehensive description of this amazing book. The Bible contains history, romance, poetry, law, and theistic doctrine among other things. However, the Bible does present a very poignant description of a very beautiful and noble woman that is well worth considering and imitating. A little disclaimer is warranted here, however. The woman I am about to describe may not be just one woman, but possibly a composite of admirable traits. It would be exhausting, if not self-defeating or impossible, to attempt to imitate exactly how the Bible describes this woman. So let's look at the following description from Proverbs 31 as a list of positive characteristics that you could include in your life and not a list of accomplishments you should seek to complete.

The 31st chapter of the book of Proverbs was written by a king named Lemuel. We don't know much more about him than that. In this chapter he relays words of wisdom given to him by his mother. The book begins with general admonitions to be kind to others, to speak up for those who have no voice, to seek justice for those who are mistreated, to care for the poor, and to avoid vices that cloud one's judgement. The bulk of this chapter, however, is a list of characteristics from Lemuel's mother on what constitutes a noble woman and how she behaves. She wants her son to choose a life partner wisely. Some people are under the impression that women in the Bible are passive, downtrodden servants of their husbands that don't speak unless spoken to. Let's look at the characteristics and traits of what a noble, beautiful woman really looks like.

She is strong. She is not a victim.

Work Ethic

Proverbs describes a woman of character as having a strong work ethic. It says she rises early in the morning and is still busy by candle light in the evening. In other words, she is not lazy. This does not mean that she works without ever resting, but idleness is not one of her character traits. She goes about her day with purpose and intentionality, not flitting from one activity to another on a whim with no goal in mind. She knows what she wants and needs to accomplish and she gets to it and stays at a task until the work is done. This includes caring for her family and employees. (That's right. This woman has women who work for her.) She is up early and ensures that her kids are fed and ready for the day. And though she has employees, she is not a harsh boss. To the contrary, she feeds them as well as her family and lays out the day's activities for them. She is caring and respectful of everyone with whom she comes in contact.

Strength

This woman Lemuel's mother describes for him is not a pushover. She is strong. She is not a victim. In fact, the author makes a point to mention her strength twice in this chapter. In verse 17 she is said to be "energetic and strong, a hard worker." The English Standard Version translation of this verse states that she "dresses herself with strength and makes her arms strong." In verse 25 she is said to be "clothed with strength and dignity." Furthermore this verse concludes that she "laughs without fear of the future." This woman is definitely not weak or passive, but courageous and strong.

A word that is not popular today but in Biblical times was often used in the description of a truly strong individual is the word meek. In today's vernacular, meekness is considered to mean passivity or weakness, a defeated submission to circumstances. In the Bible, meekness is a virtue. It is related to the taming of a strong animal. Picture a strong horse going into battle, nostrils flaring and chomping at the bit to charge. Yet he awaits the cue of his rider to unleash his fury. This is strength under control, making it useful and effective rather than haphazard and destructive. Therefore, a person who is truly strong also demonstrates meekness. They know when to use their strength and when to restrain it. Thus, their strength is slave to *them* rather than them being a slave to their emotions. Old fashioned meekness – strength under control – is the sign of a truly strong person.

Wise

Since Proverbs is a book of wisdom, it only makes sense that wisdom is a key attribute of the noble woman. This woman is wise in her business dealings. Yes, you read that correctly. In this chapter she is said to have made a real estate transaction. It says she considered a field and bought it. The woman, not her husband, made the deal. What does it mean to "consider" a field? It means she did not jump into this deal willy-nilly. She would have had to research the field to ensure the soil was fertile and not arid, thus able to produce food for her family. Was the location of the field acceptable for her purposes? Did she have the funds to purchase the land and was the asking price a good deal? Was this a good investment or should she continue looking? Thus, this woman is very intelligent in addition to being a wise business woman. Lemuel continues on to say she makes sure her business dealings are profitable. Many of today's CEOs could learn from this individual: she is able to succeed in her business dealings *and* keep her ethics intact while remaining respected by her colleagues and rivals alike.

This Proverbs 31 woman demonstrates her wisdom in choosing a mate. Her husband is known and respected in the community and by other civic leaders. This does not mean you should aim to marry a wealthy man. (I was once told by a woman with life experience under her belt that if a woman marries a man for money, she will earn every penny of it. In other words, some men of means may not be all that pleasant to live with.) The man she has chosen for a mate is, however, of strong character and respected by others. He is not lazy or foolish. He may not be a wealthy baron, but his reputation is second to none. Such a man's character flows over into his treatment of his family.

Finally, even this woman's manner of speaking is highlighted. Verse 26 states that when she speaks even her words are wise. Not only that, but her words are delivered with kindness. She is not a gabber that never takes a breath. Rather, when she speaks, what she has to say is well worth listening to. And she delivers her words with the dignity of others in mind. She is not belittling or abusive.

Confident

This strong, wise woman is also confident. Verse 18 shows that she is sure that the work of her hands is of high quality: "She perceives that her merchandise is profitable." (English Standard Version) She feels good about the fruit of her labor. She is not afraid of potential troubles to come because she has prepared for the unforeseen. She does not dread the cold weather of winter. Why? Because she was diligent and made warm clothing for her family. Confidence does not mean cockiness in this context. She has simply objectively assessed that she has prepared for the future and is satisfied with her readiness. The only hint of arrogance is when she laughs at the future. She is not being smug here. She simply does not fear the future because she feels prepared to take it head on.

She is sure that the work of her hands is of high quality.

Kind

Some people confuse strength and self-assuredness with an aggressive nature. This woman is not mean or gruff or loud or overbearing at all. She does not force her agenda ahead of others'. In fact, she is said to be exceedingly kind. Not only does she care for her own family, she helps the poor and reaches out to the needy. And, as mentioned earlier, she treats her workers with respect, rather than lording it over them and is said to give instructions with kindness. This is where true confidence comes into play. A person, who is self-assured and confident in their abilities, can be gentle in their interactions with others because they don't feel they have to prove anything to anybody. They are comfortable with themselves and they like who they are.

Respected

By virtue of this woman's very nature and all the attributes she displays and her interactions with others, she is respected by everyone that her life touches. Let's start with her husband. Not only does her husband trust her implicitly, he is quite frankly in awe of her. He trusts her to take the family funds and purchase a piece of land and conduct business. He has no fear that she will cheat on him with another man. And for this he praises her. He lauds her with compliments. He tells her that there are many amazing women in the world, but she beats them all. Her husband is telling her that out of all the women in the world he would choose her any day of the week and twice on Sunday. And why shouldn't he? We are told in verse 11 that she greatly enriches his life! Lemuel's mother tells him that such a woman is a rare find indeed and that a man who can marry such a woman has found something "more precious than jewels." She has immeasurable value.

Even this woman's children are said to stand and bless her. They don't talk back to her in a disrespectful manner, because they can see that she is strong and wise and loving and they respect her for that. This chapter closes by stating that such a woman will be rewarded for all the good she has done and for her character and for how she conducts herself. We are told to give someone like this her due. She does not have to convince anyone of her noble character because her deeds and good works speak for themselves. Strength of character, kindness, and wisdom have resulted in sincere respect from all who know her.

Physical Appearance

Now I have an assignment for you. I want you to put this book down and grab a Bible. Turn to Proverbs 31 and read verses 10-31. No, don't skip this part. Go get a Bible and open it to Proverbs 31. As you read, I want you to jot down everything you can find out about this woman's physical appearance. What does she look like? What color of hair does she have? How tall is she? What color of skin does she have? What is her makeup like? What kind of jewelry is she wearing? What does her body look like? Now go do it. No cheating and reading ahead without completing this assignment.

So what did you find? Nothing, right? That seems odd. We are taught to focus on beauty. Reporters congregate on the red carpet at Hollywood award shows to document how gorgeous all the stars are and "who" they are wearing. They want to know who did their makeup and hair. Women are led to believe that they should have 6-pack abs and be able to pose on the cover of the *Sports Illustrated* swimsuit issue without any photo shopping or airbrushing. We've already determined that the depictions on the covers of magazines don't actually exist in the real world without a lot of doctoring and manipulation of the photos. So why are this Proverbs 31 woman's looks never mentioned?

Verse 30 sums it up: Charm is deceptive and beauty does not last. It doesn't last! How many times have we seen gorgeous stars of

A BEAUTIFUL WOMAN

yesteryear plastered on issues of tabloids or on the internet under headings like, "What They Look Like Without Makeup," or, "What Do They Look Like Now?" We age. Things sag and wrinkle. Our outer appearance will change, and usually not for the better. But our inner self can remain and, indeed, grow even more beautiful as the years go by. I don't know if Mother Teresa was ever on the cover of Vogue, but who hasn't heard of Mother Teresa? She was the definition of "good." She gave and loved and was kind to the lowliest of the low and those who had been cast aside by society. Yet this beautiful woman was strong when she needed to be. Though small in stature, Mother Teresa was a titan when she testified on the world stage on behalf of these throw-away people. She was a giant and is still known and revered today.

Let me make a prediction: Beyoncé will one day be featured in one of those, "What Do They Look Like Now," articles when her beauty succumbs to time. If she has a strong, admirable character and makes positive contributions to the lives of others and society as a whole, those traits will outshine the effects of aging. Let me use another example. Tim Tebow – yes, I realize he is not a woman, but stick with me here – is a young, good looking, muscular, hunky guy. He played college football, was a stud quarterback, won the Heisman trophy and two National Championships. Before he was married, Tim had the world by the tail and could have gotten any woman he wanted. But one day time is going to catch up with him too. The muscles will atrophy. He may get a belly and gray hair or have no hair at all. But I have a feeling nobody will notice those physical traits because his character looms larger than life. This good looking, beefcake of a man has always given back to the less fortunate. You can find videos of him all over the internet caring for orphans, giving his time to kids with disabilities – real meaningful, face-time, not self-aggrandizing photo-ops that serve him only. He has a foundation that, among other things, arranges a prom night for high school kids with various disabilities. People put on a great night for these kids that they might otherwise never enjoy. The girls get all dolled up, the boys dress up and they are treated like royalty for one night. And Tim shows up! He escorts these girls into their prom. He dances with them. He has a huge smile on his face as he is bouncing to the music right smack-dab in the middle of all the kids, just like he was one of them. This is a guy who could have dominated the club scene in any major American city, taking home any woman he pleased, but instead, he chose to party with these kids who other people overlooked. Tim's positive character will outshine any deterioration in his physical appearance over time. And he is just getting warmed up. I believe Tim's character and contributions in the lives of others will continue to grow exponentially, and for that he will be remembered as a great person, not because of what he looks like.

Work on your character. Character will last. Looks and beauty will not. We know nothing about the physical appearance of our lady in the 31st chapter of the book of Proverbs, but we do know she was strong, and smart and wise and respected and beloved by her kids, her husband and everyone she touched during her lifetime. That is what real beauty looks like.

Don't Try to be Superwoman

A BEAUTIFUL WOMAN

Like I mentioned earlier in this chapter, the description that is presented in Proverbs 31 may not be one actual woman but, rather, a list of positive attributes and characteristics of truly beautiful women. It would be exhausting if not impossible to attempt to precisely imitate this woman. I mean, just look at what she is said to have been on any given day: a wife, a mother, a real estate mogul, a farmer, a seamstress, a business owner, a manager, and an importer. Sheesh! No one could do all that and do it well. So don't try to copy her literally. But look at her character traits: strength, kindness, love, intelligence, industriousness, positive dealings with others. And look to emulate those things. Don't get me wrong, it is not wrong to take pride in your appearance, to look your best and to take care of your outward appearance. But don't do so at the expense of your inner being. Don't neglect building up the characteristics that will make you a truly beautiful woman well after your exterior begins to age. Your interior is more valuable than your exterior because that is where true beauty comes from.

INCOMPARABLE

Things to Think About

1) What attributes or characteristics do you admire about the woman in Proverbs 31?

   How could you begin to incorporate some of those attributes into *your* daily life?

2) This woman is comfortable with the person she is and she likes who she is.

   Do you like who you are?

   If you do not, what would need to happen for you to like who you are?

3) In today's world people *demand* to be respected. The woman in Proverbs 31 never demanded respect; nonetheless, she was greatly respected by her family, friends, and peers because of who she was and how she treated others, as well as how hard she worked.

   Do you feel people respect you?

A BEAUTIFUL WOMAN

The one person you have control over is you. Do *you* respect yourself? If not, why?

What would it take for you to begin respecting yourself?

Since you cannot control how anyone thinks except yourself, perhaps this is an excellent place to start. Gain your own respect first.

4) While we can improve our outer appearance, Proverbs shows us that our character has unlimited potential for improvement, and this is wholly under our control. Furthermore, our inner self (our character) is what makes us beautiful and worthy of respect.

Does this change how you see your potential? How so?

Chapter 8:

What Does Love Look Like?

How many books, poems, sonnets, plays, movies, songs, and letters have been written about love and romance? I wouldn't even venture a guess. I doubt anyone would be able to tell us. Try entering the word "love" into an internet search engine and see if you can count as high as the number of entries that are returned.

So what is love? Trying to define love seems like a daunting task. Romance novels and music lead us to believe love is an intense feeling for another person. Certainly warm, fuzzy, exciting feelings are a wonderful part of "falling in love" with someone. But people will tell you they "love" certain foods or sports or seasons or activities or…. the list could go on forever. Are the feelings one has for a car or a piece of jewelry the same as the feelings for another human being? Are feelings for inanimate objects as legitimate as those for a person? And who has the knowledge or the right to define what love is for other people? There appear to be more questions than answers about what love actually is. So let's look at some descriptions of love.

Hollywood has made loads of money from producing movie after movie about a hot leading man winning the heart of a beautiful woman, or forbidden love between two characters. For decades the movie industry has provided romantic comedies and tragedies and movies with perfect happily-ever-after endings to entertain and leave viewers crying or awestruck. Before film, authors filled page after page with love stories going clear back to Shakespeare and further. Frequently these forms of media portray love as a feeling that affects us deeply. Such feelings of love can make us grin uncontrollably from ear to ear as well as cause us to forgo food and curl up in agony and cry until we have no tears left. Such intense emotions can cause us to do things we would not otherwise do, because of our state of mind brought about by the effects of such feelings. Feelings of love can cause us to say even crazier things.

We have been told: love is a many splendored thing; love is the answer; love is forever; love knows no bounds; love is scary; love is an action; love is rare; love is in the air; love is selfless; love is tolerant; love is kind; love is hard; love is easy; love is like quicksand; love is all there is, and on and on we could go. So what are we to believe? Let's look at some illustrations of what real love looks like before we answer that question.

But I will

Alfred sat contentedly in the room next to her bed. No words were exchanged. In fact she slept most of the time. The only sounds in the room were the ticking of the clock on the wall and the rhythmic rocking of his chair as he passed the time with a smile on his face. Why shouldn't he smile? He was with the love of his life.

Alfred was the president of a university. "Was" is the key word. Alfred recently walked away from a career he loved in addition to an enviable salary. After a career in education he had attained the top job at his alma mater. He ran the campus he used to roam as a bright and much younger college student many moons ago. He had steadily worked his way up the success ladder until he landed the front parking spot, the car provided him, and the beautiful home owned by the university. But that was all in the past now. And he had no regrets.

His beautiful bride, Margaret, was his only concern now. They had been together since their freshman year in college and he wasn't about to leave her now. Several years ago Margaret began having trouble remembering names and then it became more difficult for her to find the right word to finish a sentence. Steadily her memory began slipping as she continued sliding into the grips of Alzheimer's disease. Gradually she lost the ability to care for herself. The most painful day for Alfred came when Margaret no longer recognized him. They had been through so much over their fifty years together. They had laughed and cried, hugged and argued, and all along the way they had woven together a wonderful tapestry of life filled with joy and memories. But now he was a stranger to his best friend and lover and the memories were as if they had never happened. Nonetheless, Alfred remained by her side, rocking and smiling as he reminisced about their adventures together.

When Alfred announced he was stepping down from his prestigious job, friends, family, and co-workers had tried to talk him out of it. Resigning his post as president would not stop the progression of his wife's disease, they reasoned. And what would he do with himself? He thrived on the challenges and excitement of the academic environment. But Alfred's mind was made up. His commitment was to Margaret.

There came a gentle knock at the door and his good friend and colleague, Tom, poked his head into the room. Alfred stood and walked across the room welcoming him with a hearty hand shake and a smile. He motioned Tom to a chair next to his. Tom inquired about Margaret and Alfred told him nothing much had changed. Their conversation did not stir her. After an exchange of some pleasantries and other small talk, Tom revealed the real reason for his visit today.

"Alfred, won't you consider coming back to the school in your former position? We could use your leadership and it would be so good for you. It might take your mind off things."

Alfred smiled and replied, "I have made my decision, Tom. I don't regret it. Margaret needs me now. The school will get along fine without me."

"But Alfred," Tom continued, "with all due respect to Margaret, in her condition she will never know if you aren't here for a few hours each day."

With a firm resoluteness, Alfred replied, "But I will." Tom had not expected this answer. "I made a commitment to Margaret the day I married her that I would be with her until the end. And I meant it. There is no way I could work knowing I had betrayed her trust whether she realized it or not." Alfred then smiled, took Margaret's hand and continued rocking as content as ever.

The Race

Abby bent down to tie her shoe laces for what must have been the fortieth time. She was so ready to run this race, she was about to grab the starter's gun and fire it herself just to get the show on the road. Abby loved to run as long as she could remember. And she was fast. As a little girl it didn't take her long to realize she could beat any kid in her neighborhood, including the boys. She found an outlet for that speed when she tried out for the junior high track team. Success came easy to her. She rarely lost a race. When Abbey got to high school a seasoned coach, once a college track star himself, spotted her talent and her love for the sport of running. He took her under his wing and set her up with an advanced conditioning program, skill development, and tutoring that could take her to the next level. And soar to the next level she did. Abbey had earned a full scholarship to a division one university where she could get a degree and discover how far she could ride this train to track stardom, perhaps even to the Olympics.

Today was her final high school event before moving onto the collegiate level. The warm May sunshine brightened a perfect spring day as she waited for her race, the 400-meter run. Abby was the odds-on favorite to take first place and, like a stallion in the starting gates at the Kentucky Derby, she was chomping at the bit to prove it to the world.

Finally, the racers were called to the starting line. The other runners looked nervous, but not Abby. She had focused and trained for this very moment and was quite confident in her abilities. She went right to her blocks and began getting her feet set. It was as if time stopped for Abby. She focused only on the track ahead and the sound of the starter's commands: "On your mark! Get set!" Bang! The gun was fired, and it was on. Abby exploded out of her stance. It took a lot of discipline to not surge ahead of the pack like she wanted to, but her coach knew she was a strong finisher and taught her to hang back in the pack until the final turn where Abby turned on the afterburners and left everyone else in her wake. It was her signature move.

The group of runners began to thin some as the slower contestants fell behind. Abby hung several spots back biding her time. In the back stretch fatigue began to show on the girls in the lead, but not Abby. She was just about to hit her stride. They rounded the back corner of the track and it was time. Abby kicked into another gear that the other runners did not possess as she made her move. She would once again stand on the medal stand in first place to finish out her high school career as the fastest girl in the state. But just as she started to explode, another girl three runners ahead of Abby twisted her ankle awkwardly, screaming out in pain as she hit the track. The other girls tried to get around her or over her but it happened so fast and one runner grazed the fallen girl with her spikes leaving a wicked gash on her leg that began to bleed instantly.

Abby could have easily hurdled the injured girl and won the race as planned, but instead she stopped. She knelt down beside the fallen girl as the other runners continued on. Abby asked if the injured girl thought she could finish the race. The girl in the grass looked up at Abby, dumbfounded. An expression that was somewhere between a grimace and a smile spread across the injured girl's face as Abby helped her to her feet. The girls wrapped an arm around each other and together, Abby lending support to off load the injured runner's painful leg, they crossed the finish line in last place. Abby would not receive a medal that day but instead, received a thundering standing ovation from a capacity crowd as the two girls embraced in true victory.

A Simple Request

As a physical therapist I see people with many varied maladies, but one elderly gentleman I had the privilege of working with very early on in my career still sticks in my mind because of the simplistic beauty of his request.

In my profession we aim to work *with* a patient in their rehabilitation by discovering what their personal goals are for therapy. What will make them view their rehab as a success? There are numerous ways to injure your shoulder and people of all ages can suffer from shoulder pain. Frequently, a loss of range of motion in the shoulder accompanies a shoulder injury. A person cannot raise their arm as high as they used to or reach behind their back as far as they were able before injuring their extremity. Each patient has their own reasons for wanting their shoulder motion back. Younger patients may want to be able to engage in athletic activities that require full shoulder range of motion. A father may want to be able to play catch with his son or daughter. Many women want to be able to reach behind their backs in order to fasten their bra. (This is no easy task and requires a good amount of motion that is sometimes very painful to regain.) The ability to toilet oneself is another skill we take for granted until we have difficulty doing it painlessly and efficiently.

Many years back, an elderly gentleman came to me for treatment for a shoulder problem. After examining him, I found he had a significant loss of motion in his shoulder making it very difficult for him to raise his arm above his head. It is easy as a physical therapist to get into the groove of a day and ask the routine question of what the patient's goals are so you can devise a plan of care to help them achieve those goals. But I had never before heard anyone answer my question of what they would like to accomplish in rehab quite the way this sweet man did. He looked at me with sad eyes as he told me that he and his wife had been married a long time. (I can't remember the exact number of years.) And each night they would each raise an arm up to their pillow where they would hold hands as they fell asleep. He couldn't do that because of his shoulder pain. After so many years together with his wife, this man still wanted to be able to hold his bride's hand as he drifted off to sleep at night. Such a seemingly simple, yet beautiful request. True love can indeed stand the test of time.

High School Sweethearts at 70

I once was around this patient another physical therapist was working with. I never worked with him, but I could hear the conversations at times in the area where he was receiving treatment. His wife would accompany him to physical therapy and they were both in their 70's. This gentleman apparently had some longstanding disease that no one had been able to pinpoint; however, it affected his strength, making it difficult to walk and making him prone to falling. One day I overhead this man's wife ask the therapist if she could take some pictures of the treatment session. She said to her husband, "Oh honey, your granddaughters will never believe the positions you are getting into," and both the man and his wife laughed like carefree kids. Later on, as I stepped into the office that faced the parking lot, I saw this husband and wife walking to their car after leaving physical therapy. He walked cautiously with his walker as his wife held onto the gait belt around his waist in case he stumbled. When therapists hold onto a patient in this manner it looks clinical. These two looked like two high school kids holding hands. They would look at each other and talk and laugh all the way to the car. She was not bothered one bit by helping her husband and he was not offended at her help. The love that flowed between the two of them was palpable and nearly visible.

The Good Samaritan

Most of us have heard the story of the Good Samaritan in one form or another, but let's take a closer look at it. A Jewish man was traveling alone when he was attacked my other men, robbed, beaten, and left for dead. As he lay there beside the road three other travelers came along at different times. The first man to come along was a priest. How would we expect a priest to react to such a situation? We would expect him to show compassion and help the man, wouldn't we? Not this one. He actually crossed over to the other side of the road and walked right past the dying man. The second man was an assistant in the Temple. Why is this important to note? The Temple was a central part of a Jewish person's life. It would not be unreasonable for a Jew to expect that someone from a Temple would lend him aide, especially when he lay dying by the side of the road. That didn't happen. The assistant also tip-toed over to the other side of the road and hurried by the injured man. So two Jews walked by their fellow man in his time of need.

WHAT DOES LOVE LOOK LIKE?

A third man came upon the injured man: a Samaritan. Jews and Samaritans hated one another with a capital H. It would not be unexpected for a Samaritan to avoid even speaking to a Jew, much less lend a helping hand. But what did this Samaritan do? He treated the Jewish man's wounds and bandaged him up. He then put him on his donkey and took him to an inn and cared for him there. The Samaritan man had business to take care of but the Jewish man was not ready to travel yet. So did the Samaritan kick the Jew to the curb because he was an inconvenience? Nope. He prepaid the innkeeper to care for the man in his absence and told him he would pay him any extra expenses the innkeeper incurred when he returned from his business trip. So which of these men showed the Jewish man love? I can't say if the Samaritan man had warm, fuzzy feelings for the Jew, but he did show real love by his act of compassion.

So What *Does* Real Love Look Like?

Love and lust generally get mixed up with one another. Lust seeks to fulfill a need or want for ourselves. Lust is self-seeking. We may feel that we "love" someone because we desire so strongly to be with them and hold them and kiss them. But such desires are for our own benefit. Lust is self-absorbed if not selfish. Real love on the other hand is completely *un*selfish and is directed towards another person for their own good. The study notes in the Tyndale Life Application Study Bible state that a person who shows real love has set aside their own natural desires in order to act in loving ways without expecting anything in return. Such love can only be acquired with the help of God himself who *is* love.

INCOMPARABLE

Love is patient and kind. Love is not jealous or boastful or proud or rude. It does not demand its own way. It is not irritable, and it keeps no record of being wronged. It does not rejoice about injustice but rejoices whenever the truth wins out. Love never gives up, never loses faith; it is always hopeful and endures through every circumstance.

1 Corinthians 13:4-7

Remember *A Charlie Brown Christmas*? When Linus gets done reading the Christmas story, what does he say to Charlie Brown? "That's what Christmas is all about, Charlie Brown." I could say to you after reading the above passage, "That's what love is all about." Read it again. And again. It is going to be hard to comprehend that kind of love because it seems so foreign to us after we have been incorrectly taught what love looks like. Imagine a love that is never mean or jealous and never loses faith in you. Can you? That is what God tells us real love is though. And that is how He loves us. He keeps no record of our wrongs. He is always hopeful for us, hopeful that we will turn to Him and love Him back. Wouldn't it be awesome to be loved like that? What if you started the trend by showing that kind of love to someone else? How might that make them feel? Just imagine how it would make you feel to be loved unconditionally.

WHAT DOES LOVE LOOK LIKE?

Things to Think About

1) If someone asked you what love is, what would you tell them?

2) Do you believe the stories above could happen in this world? Why or why not?

3) Read 1 Corinthians 13:4-7 above again and write down what is says love looks like.

4) Is there someone you could show love to today simply by asking them how they are doing or feeling today? Is there something you could do for them that would make them feel as if you cared for them, that they were loved? If so, what is stopping you from doing it?

Chapter 9:

How Should a Woman Expect to be Treated by a Man?

Is chivalry dead? Is respect outdated? Are gentlemen extinct? Perhaps *I* am outdated or have no shred of 'cool' left in me, but it appears that women are looked upon as mere objects of pleasure on demand by some males in our society. Some modern-day song lyrics glorify the objectification of women and misogynistic treatment by men. A few of these lyrics are so inappropriate I can't even list them in this book.

Don't get me wrong. I'm a guy. Women are beautiful. Songs and poems have been written about their beauty for centuries. But lately the lyrics have become base and lewd. (And that's an understatement.) Perhaps today's writers lack education or a vocabulary or even an imagination. But ordering a woman you admire to "Back that *@# up!" just isn't going to capture the attention of a quality woman, guys. Wooing a lady by touching her heart appears to be a lost art. And, I would guess, this is sadly missed and greatly desired by women of all walks of life. Maybe men are simply too lazy and don't want to put any effort into winning the affections of the fairer sex.

You will get attention, but for all the wrong reasons.

Ladies, don't be too quick to cast all the blame on men, however. Some of you need to take a second or third look in the mirror before you leave the house. I have seen more discreet visuals of the human body in the pages of anatomy books than what I see parading around in public somedays. You make scantily clad blush. Honest to God ladies, I want to shake some of you and say, "Stop giving it away for free!" Because that is exactly what you are doing. Sure you will get attention, but for all the wrong reasons. Let me share a little secret with you about men: we are opportunists; we will take the easiest route to get what we want. But I can almost guarantee you, men who notice you in your barely-there dress or transparent leggings don't respect you and they aren't viewing you as a woman they want to establish a long-term relationship with. They see you as an easy target. They know they will not have to work to gain your affections. They are like hunters that see an easy meal. So cover up a little ladies! I'm not suggesting you can't accentuate the beauty that females are blessed with, but if Cardi B and Kim Kardashian are your role models, you need to find new ones. If you want respect from a man, you need to respect yourself first.

I'm going to share an extreme example of a man showing a woman he seriously wants a life with her. In chapter 29 of the book of Genesis a story is told of a man named Jacob. He fell in love with a woman named Rachel. Jacob so desired Rachel that he offered to work for her father for 7 years if he could have her hand in marriage. Rachel's father agreed. By this gesture, Rachel could easily see that Jacob was genuinely interested in her and fully committed to winning her as his life partner. He wasn't just interested in a good time. Jacob was true to his word and worked the full seven years as he had agreed. Now get this ladies, Genesis 29:20 says, "But his love for her was so strong that it seemed to him but a few days." (Okay, time out for a collective sigh and a big, "Awww.") What woman wouldn't want to be desired like that?

The story takes an odd turn though. On Rachel and Jacob's wedding night, Rachel's father pulled a trick on his son-in-law. He didn't feel it was fair for his younger daughter, Rachel, to get married before her older sister, Leah. So their father slipped his older daughter, Leah, into Jacob's tent that night, unbeknownst to the groom. There were no electric lights back then so poor Jacob consummated the marriage with Rachel's older sister. Jacob was obviously angry in the morning for the deception by his father-in-law. So the girls' father gave Rachel to Jacob as his wife also on the condition that Jacob work another seven years. Jacob gladly consented.

Am I saying you should look for a man who is willing to work 14 years for you (and marry your sister)? No. But you do want a man who is willing to demonstrate his commitment and love for you. Don't sell yourself short ladies. And don't settle for a lazy man who is only out for a good time or a short-term relationship. In the animal world there is a species of duck known as the wood duck. The female wood duck chooses her mate, NOT the other way around. The male wood ducks preen for the female wood duck's attention. They have to sell themselves to *her*. So what kind of values should you be looking for in a man? (Men, if you happen to be reading this, pay attention.)

What to look for in a man

1) You should be attracted to him. We aren't looking for a household appliance or a car here. We are not looking for simply dependable and low maintenance. We are looking for a love interest. Thus, he should interest you. To be sure, outward appearance is not everything, but there should be a spark between you and him.

2) He should treat you with respect. This is important. If you respect yourself, it is completely appropriate to expect mutual respect from a potential mate. What are some examples of mutual respect you might look for? He should be on time when he makes a date with you or meets you somewhere. This tells you that he views your time as valuable. Unexpected situations arise and people are late sometimes. That's life. But overall, a man who respects you as a person does not keep you waiting on a regular basis. A man who respects a woman may open doors for her. There are varied social norms today and, while this is not a deal breaker, it sure is nice and conveys concern for the other person. A person who respects you will listen to you with attention. He will look you in the eye and allow you to finish your thought before responding. He won't be checking his

watch or phone when you are trying to convey something of importance to him.

3) He backs off when you say, "NO!" (We are talking about when he attempts to cross the line romantically. I don't mean that you get to demand you get your way with every decision from which restaurant to eat at or which movie to watch. Those require compromise at times in healthy relationships.) A man who is truly interested in you in the long term is able to show physical affection by holding your hand or giving you a hug without expecting more.

4) A man who is worth your time will speak to you with respect. He will not be harsh, or threatening or condescending. This form of communication goes both ways, remember.

5) A man who is truly interested in you will try to keep you interested in him. He will clean up and not dress sloppily. A man who is pursuing a woman will want to look and smell nice for her. He will do nice things for you, such as leave a voice mail or text just to let you know he is thinking of you. Not every man is great with words, so a sonnet is not necessary. But he should remind you in his own way that you are important and matter to him.

Karla, a friend of mine I used to work with once told me a story I believe every woman should hear. In high school Karla was not getting asked out on dates. She was obviously quite disappointed, hurt, and confused by this. So one day, Karla confided in her older brother who shared with her a great truth that encouraged her so much she remembers it to this day after 20-plus years of marriage. Karla's brother could see that his little sister was truly saddened by her lack of suitors. So he sat her down and told her, "Karla, there are two types of girls: girls you date and girls you marry. You are the marrying kind." Karla is a beautiful woman. What her brother told her helped her realize that she was a quality female and the lazy boys who wanted easy affection without working for it would not ask her out because they realized she was not "that kind of girl." She was the type of girl they would one day want to build their life around. At that age, however, these were simply immature, lazy high school boys. They weren't ready for a lifetime commitment, and, speaking as a man, these boys were probably intimidated by a mature, beautiful, quality girl. Her brother's explanation also made Karla realize she was avoiding inevitable heartache and perhaps degrading treatment by immature little boys.

Another piece of this story came out later in Karla's married life. Her now husband went to the same high school as Karla. After they had been married awhile, Karla's husband told her that he had wanted to save her for himself one day, so he would tell the other boys in school that Karla was cold, prudish and not easy, though he had no personal knowledge of such, just so he would deter the other boys from asking Karla out. That's kind of a crummy way of going about it, but her husband realized Karla was a girl of excellence he would one day like to build a life with and he didn't want to risk any of the other boys winning her heart before he did.

So what kind of woman do you want to be: the kind men date then toss aside when they get what they want from you or the kind with whom they want to build a life together? It truly is your choice. Remember, you are a masterpiece created by an Artisan that loves

INCOMPARABLE

you deeply and values you immeasurably. You are priceless. Look for a man who feels the same about you.

HOW SHOULD A WOMAN EXPECT TO BE TREATED BY A MAN?

Things to Think About

1) In the past, how have you been treated by men/boys?

2) Do you feel this treatment was appropriate? Why or why not?

3) If God sees you as a masterpiece, then how do you think men or boys should treat you?

4) List out one or two things that would make you feel respected by a man or boy.

   What if a man/boy does not do these things? What can you do in such a situation to show respect to yourself?

Chapter 10:

So What Do You Do With All This

God Stuff?

Someone recently asked me what important piece of wisdom I would pass on to someone younger than me. It only took me a couple seconds to come up with an answer because it is something I would love every fellow human being to consider as if their very life depended on it - because it does.

One day each of us will close our eyes for the last time on this earth. Some believe when that occurs our eyes stay shut forever. They believe there is nothing more after death. Some believe there is life after death, and others believe there is a God we meet after we die.

Eons ago, a scientist and philosopher named Blaise Pascal proposed that every person bets with his or her life whether or not God exists. He reasoned that if those who believe there is no God are correct, then they simply cease to exist once they die. On the other hand, if they are wrong about the existence of God and life after this one, Pascal posited that they will not only have made a critical error with eternal ramifications that they are unable to undo, they will have missed out on the many ways God can enhance our existence while still on this earth.

As for those who believe in God, if they are correct, they will have benefited from God's instruction on how to get the most out of this life *plus,* they will enjoy eternity with Him once this life has ended. If they are misguided in their convictions however, they will simply cease to exist but they will have enjoyed a good life by adhering to the joy producing tenets of the God they believed in. It is a win-win for the believers and a lose-lose for the skeptics.

Isn't God Just a Myth?

I can fully understand how belief in God can seem like the stuff of fairy tales. If you were not raised around these beliefs they can seem pretty strange, even nonsensical. We live in an age where scientific knowledge steadily increases and people are taught to believe only in what they can see or touch or test or prove. My profession and training are steeped in science and the scientific method. But one thing I have discovered is that science constantly changes. Not in the too distant past, when a person had surgery to repair a torn anterior cruciate ligament in their knee, the surgeon would put them in a cast for several weeks. Doing that now would be tantamount to medical malpractice as scientific discoveries have uncovered more effective ways to help these patients recover and return to function. In fact, the rehabilitation process has improved significantly over the years as science has progressed. Science constantly changes and has revealed flaws in our knowledge base over the years, just as the example above demonstrates. What is written in the Bible, however, has remained the same for thousands of years and continues to be proven correct over and over again.

I was raised by parents who took me and my brothers to church. We learned about the Bible and the Christian faith at an early age.

Thus, I can understand how learning about it as an adult in this day and age of science and technology and skepticism would make believing more difficult. However, I don't believe in the person of Jesus Christ, that he actually is who he claims he is, simply because I learned about him as a child. The more I study the Bible and history and science, the more convinced I become of the realities of God. Some people believe Jesus Christ was a good teacher or a philosopher, a myth or a kook or a master manipulator. But the odds that he is NOT the son of God are astronomical to the point of making this conjecture an impossibility. What do I mean? There are many prophecies (predictions) in the Old Testament of the Bible about what the Messiah would be like, where he would be born, when he would be born, how he would die, etc. Peter Stoner, professor of mathematics and astronomy, authored a book, *Science Speaks*, where he calculated the odds that any one person could fulfill just 8 of these predictions to be 1 in 10^{17}. That is 1 with 17 zeros after it. I don't even know the name of that number.

What is written in the Bible has remained the same for thousands of years and continues to be proven correct over and over.

Professor Stoner explains this number in an easy-to-understand way. He asks us to imagine filling the entire state of Texas with silver dollars to the depth of 2 feet deep across the entire land mass of the state. Then imagine he drew a red x on one of those silver dollars, randomly tossed it somewhere in the pile of coins, then stirred the entire state full of coins mixing them up. Now imagine that he put a blindfold on you, dropped you off somewhere in Texas, and allowed you to venture as far as you liked, reach down, and pull out a silver dollar from the mix and hand it to him. The odds of you selecting the coin with the red "x" on it is the same probability that any one person could fulfill just 8 of the major ancient prophecies concerning the Messiah. The man, Jesus Christ, fulfilled 61 of them! The odds of that happening are a number that is simply beyond my comprehension to even try to explain.

This man Jesus Christ was born where it was foretold the Messiah would be born. He died the way it was foretold the Messiah would die, by crucifixion. Crucifixion is a horrible, ghastly form of execution. It is described in the Old Testament book of Isaiah ....hundreds of years before crucifixion was ever invented as a means of execution! Some will try to say that Jesus Christ was a kook who wanted to be famous so he went about trying to fulfill these old prophecies. For this to happen, he would have had to influence where he was born, not to mention, coercing the Roman government at the end of his life into playing along with his charade by crucifying him. Not only that, he would have had to tell the Roman soldiers, "Hey guys, once they nail me to that cross, I want you to take my clothes and throw dice for them to see who gets to keep them. Do you think you could do that for me?" Such arguments are completely ludicrous. However, all those occurrences were written down hundreds of years before they happened. It is utterly impossible that a person could have fulfilled all these things (and the science of probability supports this claim) unless, of course, he was actually the Messiah, the Son of God. That is how facts bolster and support my faith that Jesus Christ is the Son of God and our Messiah. This is not just a childhood fantasy for me.

So What Does This Mean For You?

This man, Jesus Christ, made many bold statements about who he was. His most audacious claim, one that outrages many even today, was that he was the *only* way the human race could be reconciled to God. Jesus Christ is the only religious figure to make that claim. That statement means there is no other person or god or path of enlightenment or any amount of good works that can justify us imperfect, wicked humans to a perfect God. I know of no other world religion that makes that assertion. This historical figure, Jesus Christ, is stating unequivocally that *he* is the only way anybody, any person, any human being to ever walk this earth can be made right with the one true God. He leaves no wiggle room in his claim. There are no loopholes. This Jesus, therefore, is either incredibly narcissistic or insane or he really is who he claims to be. *That*, my friends, is the most important issue any person will ever deal with in this life. If we avoid the topic, we by default reject his claim. Don't put if off any longer if you have not dealt with it.

Think of it this way. Imagine, God forbid, you are critically ill. One physician, after examining you, looks you squarely in the eye, tells you he has seen your condition numerous times and that there is only one way, one course of treatment that will cure you and prevent you from dying. Meanwhile, other naysaying physicians tell you the first doctor is crazy and that there must be other ways to save your life, though they have never seen a patient successfully treated by these other purported interventions. Whose advice are you going to follow?

A while back I read of a Jewish man who was rebellious in his younger years. He thought he knew everything and was deeply offended when someone challenged him by saying Jesus Christ was the Messiah the Jewish people had been waiting for. One day someone challenged this man to read the Bible and see for himself. Since the Jewish faith does not recognize the New Testament of the Bible, the man further challenged the Jewish young man to read only the texts of the Old Testament his faith accepted. There was just one caveat: each time the Jewish man sat down to read he was to ask God to show him if this Jesus was real even though he did not believe in Him. The more the man read, the more it became glaringly obvious that the texts of his own Jewish faith in the Old Testament of the Bible had been pointing all along to this Messiah, Jesus Christ, who had already come to save all mankind nearly 2000 years ago. In his excitement at this new knowledge, the Jewish man began to read the New Testament and was overwhelmed at how the proof of this predicted Messiah was found in Jesus Christ.

I lay down the same challenge for you. But simply begin with the book of John. Find a Bible and read through this book of John in the New Testament. Take hours, days or weeks. However, each time before you read tell God that you don't know if you believe in Him or Jesus or any of this "religious" stuff. Then ask Him to reveal the truth to you as you read, and see what happens.

What Then?

If, after having examined the evidence, you conclude that this Jesus Christ really is the Savior of the world you are very close to eternal life. In the tenth chapter of the book of Romans in verses 9 and 10 we are told:

> *If you confess with your mouth that Jesus is Lord and believe in your heart that God raised him from the dead, you will be saved. For it is by believing in your heart that you are made right with God, and it is by confessing with your mouth that you are saved.*
> Romans 10:9-10

It gets better though. Verse 13 of that same chapter of Romans says:
> *Everyone who calls on the name of the Lord will be saved.*
> Romans 10:13

And do you know what the Biblical meaning of the word *everyone* is in this verse? Everyone! You, me, the person next to you, that lady across the country.... Anyone and everyone who truly believes that Jesus Christ is who He says he is and wants to be saved, not only from eternal separation from Him when we die but also from our wretched life now, can be. Many people believe there must be more to salvation. However, salvation is all about Jesus Christ, not about us. In other words, He has done all the work. He paid the price. We did nothing. He has provided salvation and eternal life as a gift. All we have to do is accept it.

SO WHAT DO YOU DO WITH ALL THIS GOD STUFF?

True belief in Christ and His gift of eternal life brings about tangible changes in a person. We will no longer want to continue in our former way of living. We will want to live God's way. Just be prepared. God is perfect. We are human and we will fall far short of perfection many, many times. God, however, is gracious and kind and patient and forgiving. He will help us along through this life in spite of our imperfections. So if a person truly believes that Jesus Christ is who He says He is – the Son of God who gave up everything to pay our penalty with His own life- he will be saved.

If you know in your heart that Jesus Christ is the true Messiah, the Savior of the world, let Him know. You can use your own words or a version of the following:

"God, thank you so much for giving up Your own Son to pay the penalty for my wrongdoing and bridging the gap between me and You. I realize this is a gift that I did not earn and I can never repay. I believe with all my heart that Jesus Christ died in my place and You raised Him from the dead thus defeating death. I accept this gift You are offering. I want to change my ways and live life Your way. Please help me. I can't do it on my own. Thank you, God, and thank you Jesus. "

God tells us that when we believe and accept His gift of salvation He adopts us as His very own sons and daughters. If you have indeed decided to follow Jesus Christ, welcome to a very big and very loving family, now and for all eternity.

Things to Think About

1) Do you believe that a man named Jesus Christ once lived, was executed, then brought back to life so we could live forever with Him?

   If you do not believe this, list out your reasons why you don't believe this.

2) Are you willing to take the challenge I laid down earlier: to read through the book of John asking Jesus to show you if He is real?

   What have you got to lose?

Chapter 11:
Living Fearlessly

Pretend you are a young kid again heading to school where you know the bully that daily torments you is waiting. Now imagine you have an older brother who is the strongest kid in school, revered and admired by every other student. And he is walking with you. Would that change how you feel? Would you be worried about the bully any longer? I doubt it. Nobody is going to mess with you because your brother is right beside you.

What would it feel like to live without fear? How liberating would that be? Imagine how stress-free and confident you would feel if fear did not have a hold on you. When you are an adopted, full-fledged member of God's family, it is possible to live at peace without fear of the future when you tap into the power of God's Spirit that resides in each of His children. When you become a member of this family, that Spirit takes up residence within you and is with you every step of the rest of your life. So what does this power look like anyway?

The Power of God

Here is how the author of Proverbs 30 describes God's power:

Who holds the wind in his fists? Who wraps up the oceans in his cloak? Who has created the whole wide world?

Not only did this Being create the whole world, He has complete control over all the elements in the universe. Think of how destructive the wind of a tornado or a hurricane can be. God holds those winds in His fists and can cast them anywhere He likes or restrain them at will. Have you ever seen what the ocean looks like during a horrible storm? He controls the power of the oceans as well. He is power personified. Christ simply spoke and storms and seas obeyed His voice and ceased their churning. Job described hearing God speak once and said it was like thunder rolling across the earth. He said it is impossible to even imagine how great His power is. Isaiah once came into the presence of God and was so overwhelmed by His power and majesty that he exclaimed, "It's all over! I'm doomed."

Is Christ a Pacifist

I believe some view Christ as a bearded, long-haired, milquetoast prophet who sat by the side of the road and let people kick sand in His face. Kind of a wimp. This depiction is very far from the truth. One term used in the Bible that could describe Him is meek. As mentioned earlier, the word meek does not mean a wimpy pushover in the Bible. It refers to restrained power.

In the equine world a bit is placed in the mouth of a horse so the rider can control the animal. Many years ago, when horses were used in times of war this bit allowed a soldier to hold his horse in check until it was time to unleash this powerful beast and allow it to go racing into battle. In a similar manner, Christ held back His power because He had a job to do. Had He let His full power rip in all its fury while He was on this earth, specifically while hanging on a cross being tortured and mocked, He never would have paid our penalty and we would be eternally lost.

...one intimidating picture of power and victory.

Now contrast this restraint of power with how Revelation 19 describes what Christ will look like one day in the future when He returns to this earth to exact His revenge on all that is evil. Heaven opens up and there stands a mighty white horse. (White symbolizes victory here. In other words, the final outcome of the battle that is about to be waged has already been decided.) And sitting on the back of that horse is Christ who is about to do battle with sin and evil for the final time. His eyes are described as being like flames of fire. His robe is dipped in blood and He carries a sword which He will use to defeat evil once and for all. This is not the picture of a wimp. That is one bad hombre. And right behind Him is an enormous army dressed in the finest pure, white linen, all on white stallions ready to do battle alongside Christ. That is one intimidating picture of power and victory. Such power as this is readily available to His brothers and sisters in God's family: to you and me.

What Does Living Fearlessly Look Like

INCOMPARABLE

Many years ago I was in charge of providing a worship service to nursing home residents for a local church. My job was to get volunteers to sing, teach a message, and serve communion. It was very difficult to get people to help. One year on New Year's Eve I had to arrange such a service. I knew there was no way I could find volunteers to help, and I did not know what I was going to do. As I was hauling the communion cups out to my car a gentleman in the church stopped me and asked what I was doing. I explained that I had a service to provide to nursing home residents. He then asked me if I needed any help. I just looked at him dumbfounded. Everyone avoided me when I was looking for volunteers. No one ever walked up to me and asked if I needed help. As it turned out, this man was a nurse who worked with older people, he was an ordained minister, and he played the guitar and sang. He could do the whole service all by himself! This just fell into my lap. When you are doing the work God has put on your heart to do, He is going to provide you with the tools to get it done. I had no reason to fear or worry. I just didn't realize it initially.

...you become invincible, and nothing can stop you from being the person God has planned you to be.

When you are in the family of God, you have access to His power in all situations. Proverbs 30:5 says, "He is a shield to all who come to him for protection." When we become one of God's adopted children, He marks us as His own by placing His Spirit within us, to walk with us, and protect us, every second of every day. The power that "holds the wind in his fists" lives inside every child of God. King David noted that God is with us during the darkest times of our lives. He doesn't even leave our side when we die. Does this mean we will never be in dangerous situations? Does it mean nothing fatal will ever befall a child of God? Unfortunately, no. But when we make up our mind to live out the purpose that God placed us on this earth to fulfill (and we each have a very specific purpose), God's power will protect us every step of the way and He will provide a way for us to finish the work He has given us to do. We are His children and He is our protector and enabler to help us fulfill our purpose. When you realize that you are priceless and can be fearless because of God's love and power that is not only available to you but indwells your very being, you become invincible and nothing can stop you from being the person God has planned you to be. Who is God calling you to be and what purpose does He have in store for you? An abundant, meaningful life awaits.

Things to Think About

1) Write down what it would mean to you to live without fear.

2) Is there anything you are afraid of that is preventing you from moving forward with your life?

3) What would you do differently today, tomorrow, next year… if you didn't fear those things any longer?

4) What do you think would happen if you told God about your fears and asked Him to remove them from you? Do you want to give that a try?

Prologue

Do you think God played a part in getting this book written and into your hands? Or do you feel it is simply happenstance that you are reading this book? I have another story for you.

I locked myself away in a hotel, away from any distractions, in order to finish the last chapter of this book. (An awesome snowstorm raged outside my window which made it all the more fun, but that is beside the point.) Late on Friday afternoon I wrote the final sentence of this book. I sat there in the quiet of my room, looking out at the snow still falling with a bittersweet sentiment in my mind: I was glad to have finished this book but sad that there was a need for such a book to be written.

The next morning I was reading like I try to do each morning. I had been studying the book of Psalms for several months. Now put this next piece of information in the context of the chapter I had just finished attempting to convince you that God has a grand purpose for your life. I was studying Psalm 138 and the last verse stated, "The Lord will work out his plans for my life." Did you catch that? Not only does God have a purpose for you, He will work this out if you let him.

I sat there in my hotel room, dumbfounded. I thought the book was done. But apparently God had one more thing He wanted to relay to you: He has a purpose for you and He will bring it about in your life. All I could think of was whoever He directs to read this book must be very, very special to Him. You must understand, when I write something like this, I do not take credit for the words on these pages. I pray each time I sit down to write that God will give me the words He wants to communicate to the people who will eventually read this book. You must be very special indeed.

Acknowledgments

This book would not exist had God not given me the inspiration to write and the words to put down on paper. I don't understand your choice, Father, but thank you for allowing me the privilege of being used by You in this way.

Without my upbringing, surrounded by a safety net of unconditional love, I never would have considered the possibility of writing a book. But my parents provided my brothers and me a true home where we could discover who we were and our purpose in life. And if we ever doubted, my parents would assure us of our innate value and potential. I wish you all could have met my parents. More than that, I wish every child could experience the home life my parents provided for my two brothers and me. It was truly one of the greatest blessings I have ever been given.

I want to thank Kim Christie for convincing me that this book was intended for a larger audience than I ever considered. I originally wrote this for victims of sex trafficking. You opened my eyes to the very real, widespread cancer that is abuse. You quickly became my biggest supporter in this endeavor. You taught me, inspired me, lead me, and gave me the confidence to keep going in this process. But then again, that's your forte; you inspire and encourage and lead people on a daily basis. You are an inspirational servant of God, and I could fill volumes listing all that you have brought to my life. Thank you. I love you.

And finally, Bailey Gagle. If not for you this book may very well have never seen the light of day. You convinced me that this

project could actually come to fruition and
handled much of the technological stuff never I would
have figured out.Thank you. You are already a force
to be reckoned with, and you 're just getting warmed
up.
Remember her name, world.